HEMINGWAY AND ME

LETTERS, ANECDOTES, AND MEMORIES
OF A LIFE-CHANGING FRIENDSHIP

JEFFREY LYONS

LYONS
PRESS

Guilford, Connecticut

An imprint of The Rowman & Littlefield Publishing Group, Inc.
4501 Forbes Blvd., Ste. 200
Lanham, MD 20706
www.rowman.com

Distributed by NATIONAL BOOK NETWORK

British Library Cataloguing in Publication Information available

Library of Congress Cataloging-in-Publication Data

Names: Lyons, Jeffrey, author.
Title: Hemingway and me : letters, anecdotes, and memories of a
    life-changing friendship / Jeffrey Lyons.
Description: Guilford, Connecticut : Lyons Press, 2021.
Identifiers: LCCN 2020054935 (print) | LCCN 2020054936 (ebook) | ISBN
    9781493055340 (cloth ; alk. paper) | ISBN 9781493055357 (epub)
Subjects: LCSH: Hemingway, Ernest, 1899-1961—Friends and associates. |
    Lyons, Leonard, 1906-1976—Friends and associates. | Authors,
    American—20th century—Biography. | Journalists—United
    States—Biography.
Classification: LCC PS3515.E37 Z6965 2021 (print) | LCC PS3515.E37
    (ebook) | DDC 813/.52 [B]--dc23
LC record available at https://lccn.loc.gov/2020054935
LC ebook record available at https://lccn.loc.gov/2020054936

To my parents, who gave my brothers and me a wonderful upbringing, and to my wife and children. They are the lights of my life.

FOREWORD

I GREW UP IN IRELAND, SO THE WORLD HEMINGWAY INHAB-
ited and the characters he created were unknown to me. But as I
grew older and eventually got work as an actor in this country, I
became aware of how his larger-than-life persona was so deeply
ingrained in the American psyche. Several of my roles cast me
as a man of action equipped with what are called "special skills."
Hemingway had special skills, too, though of a different sort.
Besides facing danger, himself, in war and as a hunter, he had
the uncanny ability to get to the heart of a character, and above
all be truthful. I never met Hemingway, but I would have loved
to have gone fly fishing with him: just the two of us along a
quiet stream or lake somewhere, contemplating his obsession
with the truth.

The letters and anecdotes in this book by my friend Jeffrey
Lyons were part of a remarkable friendship between Heming-
way and Jeffrey's dad Leonard. For forty years in the heyday of
New York newspapers and nightclubs, he wrote a must-read
column six days a week covering the doings of newsworthy
people from all walks of life. Carl Sandburg once said he wished
Lyons's column, "The Lyons Den," had been around during
Lincoln's time.

Leonard Lyons's friendship with Hemingway also changed
young Jeffrey's life, as one chapter of the book explains. The letters give you a sense of the man behind the legend: his likes and

dislikes, his utter disregard for authority, and his work ethic. Lyons was also privy to Hemingway's novels before any other journalist, as if they were extended stories told from one old friend to another.

There's a portion of the book about the Lyons family's visit to the Hemingway home near Havana where Jeffrey's older brother George asked him how you write a novel. "You keep your sentences short by pretending the words are being tattooed on your back," he replied. I liked that.

—Liam Neeson

PREFACE

I REMEMBER THE NIGHT OF JULY 2, 1961 AS IF IT WERE YES-
terday. It was hot, as it always is in Spain in the summer, and
the evening brought little relief. There was no breeze, but it was
still balmy. I was fifteen years old, in *La Plaza de Toros del Puerto
de Santa María*, the 12,500-seat bullring in that small city in
southwest Spain. I was standing in a place few Americans ever
get to stand, the *callejón*. I remember thinking it was the equiva-
lent of watching a major-league baseball game from the home
team's dugout. The *callejón* is the narrow passageway between
the *barrera*, the bottom of the stands, and the *burladero*, the low
wooden wall with slats which encircles the arena floor. It's the
place where bullfighters taking a rest between their appearances
and bull breeders sit or stand and watch or debate how brave
the bulls are and how skillfully the men are performing. It can
be a dangerous place, too, if the bull jumps over the barrier and
into that space, which has happened occasionally. Then chaos
breaks out as everyone scrambles to get out of the way before
the bull is lured back into the arena itself.

I knew I had an extremely rare entrée for an American, especially for a teenager, because I was traveling that summer with
Antonio Ordoñez, Spain's greatest matador of his era. My trip
had been arranged by Mary Hemingway, at the behest of her
husband Ernest, a month earlier. Mary and Ernest, good friends
of my family, had learned that ever since I saw my first bullfight

in 1956, I'd become an *aficionado*: a dedicated fan. Three years before he would write *The Manchurian Candidate*, the author Richard Condon took my father and me to a bullfight in Toledo, the ancient city about forty-five miles from Madrid. At first I was shocked, but then became transfixed. It's an indefensible addiction, especially for an animal lover like me, but there it was: A lifetime love for *La Fiesta Brava*, bullfighting was born.

I remember arriving in Madrid a week earlier, my letter of introduction in hand, at Antonio and his wife Carmen's luxurious apartment on the Calle Jerez where I was quickly welcomed into their home and eventually into their extended family. Years later, Mary Hemingway told me she and Ernest had thought my tour with Ordóñez would last two weeks or so. Little did anyone know it would last seven summers as well as twenty-eight subsequent visits and counting to Spain.

Antonio was appearing in a charity bullfight, held at night as opposed to the normal 5:00 p.m. starting time. It's been said that in Spain, the only thing which starts on time is a bullfight. Thus, instead of the customary "Suit of Lights" the *toreros* usually wear, festooned with gold for the matadors and silver for their assistants, they were dressed in *traje corto*, the familiar bolero jacket, leather chaps, and boots, with big round *sombreros*. After Antonio had faced the first of his two bulls, he stood in the *callejón* waiting his turn after the other, less senior matadors would perform. Then the shocking word came from Ketchum, Idaho, of his godfather Ernest Hemingway's sudden, tragic death.

When the bugle sounded signaling it was time for Antonio to face his second bull, he'd had about forty minutes to absorb the awful news. Then he strode to the middle of the arena, performed admirably in the early part of the ritual, then came over to get his *muleta,* the small red cape, curved sword, and hat in hand. At the other side of the arena, the bull was being distracted by his assistants. The crowd hadn't yet heard the news and wondered why he knelt to the ground on one knee in the center of the arena and said a prayer. Then the word began to spread quickly. Suddenly, as if on command, a hush spread around the arena, eerily silencing the crowd. Ordoñez slowly arose and pointed his hat to the sky, dedicating the death of the bull to his godfather.

Back in Ketchum, Mary had initially said publicly that her husband had died accidently cleaning his favorite shotgun. Subsequent reports soon emerged, however, saying that he'd been treated for depression and cancer at the Mayo Clinic, which pointed to his death being self-inflicted. His father Clarence Edmund Hemingway, a doctor in Oak Park, Illinois, had also taken his life in 1928, as would several other family members, most notably his granddaughter, actress/model Margaux Hemingway, in 1996. The family had been rife with suicides—seven in all—which prompted his younger granddaughter, actress and filmmaker Mariel, to make an anti-suicide documentary called *Running from Crazy* about it, hoping it might help.

My father was not in his usual nightclub haunts in New York that night, gathering stories for his daily Broadway column, "The Lyons Den." He'd made one of his infrequent trips to Los Angeles and was staying at the famed Beverly Hills Hotel. Before she contacted the police, Mary called our home in New York with the news. It was my sister-in-law Robin who heard the voice on the other end. "Lenny, Ernest shot himself this morning." She was then given the number of the hotel in California. My father received an early morning call and heard the operator say: "Ketchum, Idaho calling." "Papa is dead" is all Mary said to him at first. She paused, then said they'd just returned from the clinic in Rochester, Minnesota, where he'd been treated for depression with shock therapy. En route back to their home in Idaho, they'd took what she described to my father as a leisurely, five-day drive together. Her husband had felt well enough the day before to think of hunting again, and she said he'd been cleaning his gun which she said accidentally went off.

Mary then asked my father to notify the world press but to offer as few details as possible. Soon, calls began to come to my father's hotel room from around the world. Mary was already busy in Ketchum making the funeral arrangements. Thus began a very long process of going through his huge stash of papers, letters, and manuscripts she would pore through and catalog in Ketchum, Key West, Paris, and finally in Cuba. As the calls kept coming, my father began to think of their quarter-century-long friendship: the two visits he and my mother had made to their Cuban *finca*, their farm outside Havana, including the first one in 1952 with my two older brothers and me; the many nights together at the Stork Club, New York's famous posh nightclub, where luminaries came to see and be seen. And there was their memorable walk together through the streets of Paris, the city of Hemingway's youth as a member of the so-called "Lost Generation" of disaffected artists and writers after the First World War. He also thought of the many afternoons lunching together at Toots Shor's restaurant where my father would join Hemingway while making his daily rounds gathering stories for his column, and their trip to a frigid Moscow in December 1955.

Soon after the tragic news of Hemingway's sudden death reached the White House, President Kennedy issued a statement:

> *Few Americans have had a greater impact on the emotions and attitudes of the American people than Ernest Hemingway. From his first emergence as one of the bright literary stars in Paris during the twenties—as a chronicler of the "Lost Generation," which he was to immortalize—he almost single-handedly transformed the literature and the ways of thought of men and women in every country in the world.*
>
> *When he began to write—the American artist had to look for a home on the Left Bank of Paris. Today, the United States is one of the great centers of art. Although his journeys throughout the world—to France, to Spain, and even to Africa—made him one of the great citizens of the world, he ended life as he began it—in the heartland of America to which he brought renown and from which he drew his art.*

Poet Archibald MacLeish proclaimed: "Ernest Hemingway was a master of English prose, the great stylist of his generation." Playwright-humorist James Thurber called Hemingway "One of the greatest writers of this century." His death was a watershed event in American literary history.

I

If you're wondering how on earth I was able to wind up in Spain traveling with a bullfighter—indeed, *the* greatest matador of them all, according to Hemingway in *The Dangerous Summer*—it was thanks to my father. Leonard Lyons was a beloved Broadway columnist, famous in his time, who wrote a column running a thousand words a day, six days a week, for forty years to the day: May 20, 1934 to May 20, 1974. That works out to 12,478 columns, give or take. Never mind the dark movie *The Sweet Smell of Success* in which Burt Lancaster played a vicious Broadway gossip columnist. His character was a feared scoundrel spewing venom in his column against his many enemies, real or perceived. That character was based on Walter Winchell and especially the infamous journalist Westbrook Pegler as well. Definitely not my Pop.

It's been said that there are three ways you can judge how a person lived a life: what they said when they were drunk, where they donated their money to charity, and by how many mourners show up at that person's funeral. My father drank half a glass of beer before bedtime each dawn to lull himself to sleep, or on occasional social occasions, he sipped wine. He was never so much as high in his life. His favorite charity was the Damon Runyon Cancer Fund for which he served as vice president. And a *thousand* people came to my father's funeral in 1976. In his eulogy, former mayor John V. Lindsay proclaimed:

"In a business of sharks, Leonard Lyons was a prince." Indeed, he was. He gave us a remarkable start in life in countless ways.

"The Lyons Den" was a must-read daily ritual, both for New Yorkers and readers across the country in the *New York Post* and 106 other newspapers. He was read in Europe as well via the *Rome Daily American* newspaper. He was a man of his times. He flourished decades before the internet, during the "Golden Age" of New York newspapers and nightclubs. New York had nearly a dozen daily papers when the column began, and when I came of age in the 1960s, there were seven, all of which my brothers and I consumed daily.

For his millions of readers, "The Lyons Den" (ironically a name given by his rival Walter Winchell in a contest) was a daily chronicle of anecdotes and news items—never gossip—about "newsworthy people" as he called them. They came from all walks of life. Actors, painters, gangsters, royals, presidents, kings, despots, philanthropists, diplomats, sports stars, jurists, etc.—he knew them all. And they trusted him. Years after his death, for example, Mickey Mantle once came to our station at WPIX-TV where I began my career as their film and theater critic. I introduced myself to the Yankee immortal and mentioned my father who Mantle would see nightly at Toots Shor's restaurant. Mantle suddenly lost the glaze he wore when meeting the usual fan, looked up, and said: "I'll always remember that your father was the only journalist who never reported that he'd seen me drunk at Toots Shor's the night before a game." "Mickey," I replied, "I want to remember this moment."

More than one hundred thousand names appeared in the columns he wrote. Each entry—whether a one-time news item or a timeless anecdote—was carefully annotated. Besides Ernest Hemingway, his best friend was Orson Welles. Marc Chagall, in exile in New York during the war, came to our home every Friday night for kosher food. One night he looked at a painting given to us by Joan Miró, the Spanish surrealist. Chagall studied it for a few minutes, then sighed and simply said *"Drek!"* He and my father communicated in Yiddish, the international folk language of the Jewish people. My parents, children of refugees from poverty in Hungary and Romania, often spoke fluent Yiddish to each other, especially when they didn't want my brothers and me to understand. Thus, the only phrases I know translate as "Let's go!", "Be quiet!", or my favorite: "Go hit your head against the wall!" Growing up, it seemed to me that every joke a comedian told began in English but had a Yiddish punchline which of course would be lost in translation.

Sir Alfred Hitchcock came for dinner to our home one evening. He spotted a silver tray on a living room table. My father had swiped it from Hitler's desk in Berchtesgaden, aka "The Eagle's Nest" in the Bavarian Alps. He was there with the First Army press corps just as the war ended. The tray had an eagle and a swastika engraved, with the initials "A. H." flanking the eagle. Hitchcock noticed those initials and tried to "claim" the tray. My parents used that tray only to carry the most kosher foods they could find. My father also swiped the phone which was Hitler's direct line to his empty-headed mistress Eva Braun. Before leaving the compound, my father then fulfilled a longtime promise he'd made to himself in 1940: He made sure to urinate on the garish thick concrete swastikas outside the building. For good measure he left the same personal "calling card" on the rug in the main room in front of Hitler's desk.

Marlene Dietrich came to our home several times. Once it was to a party soon after someone had told my mother that they'd spotted the leggy actress having a late supper with my father at Lindy's, the famous restaurant of that era. "Oh, I'm not worried," said my mother Sylvia. "After all, Lindy's is world famous for its cheesecake."

Another guest was Joe DiMaggio. He was a favorite of Hemingway, who wrote about "The Yankee Clipper" in *The Old Man and the Sea*, published the year after DiMaggio retired. The shy DiMaggio came to our home for a party honoring the great actress Ethel Barrymore in 1950. I was five years old and was awakened by the hubbub of the guests in our living room. Walking in, I scanned the room, and spotted Joe in a corner, standing nervously by himself. Ignoring the other guests, I didn't recognize, who'd paused to watch, I walked over to DiMaggio, tugged at his jacket, looked up at him, and said: "Mr. DiMaggio, you're the best guest here." At an Old-Timers' Game at Yankee Stadium in 1973, he asked me if I'd still say that about him.

Years later, I learned that the other guests in our living room I'd breezed past that night included Adlai Stevenson, who two years later ran the first of two campaigns for president, movie star Edward G. Robinson, the aforementioned Marlene Dietrich, Broadway songwriters Comden and Green, and Ernest Hemingway.

In 1990, I took our son Ben to a baseball card show where Joe was signing cards, bats, and balls and sent word up to the stage that we were there and wanted to greet him. He stopped the long line, pushed me aside, put his arm around then-nine-year-old Ben and they talked for about ten minutes. "Dad," said Ben later, "Mr. DiMaggio told me what you were like at my age."

Other visitors to our home included John Steinbeck and Nobel Peace Prize winner and UN undersecretary-general Ralph Bunche. Besides helping settle the 1948 Arab-Israeli war, one evening he also settled a "Lyons Brothers' War" over who got to use the newly acquired TV by flipping a coin! This was the unusual childhood I had. Since he wasn't a baseball player, to me at the time, Hemingway was just another of my parents' many friends.

The column was a daily relentless grind for my father. Unlike his competitors in the dozen other newspapers, he used no "leg man": no assistant besides a secretary. He got the exclusive news items and anecdotes himself in twice-daily rounds of restaurants and nightclubs. In those days, they were always filled with newsworthy people. The column was the key to everything: movie premieres, Broadway opening nights, tea with the Churchills at 10 Downing Street, dinner with the Trumans on their last night in the White House, visits to movie sets and Hollywood and London, lunching at studio moguls' offices, and nightly encounters with the luminaries of his era. And friends like Orson Welles and the Sofia Loren and the Hemingways.

He'd take my three brothers and me to really special places: the palace in Monaco where we were greeted by Princess Grace, his old friend from her days in New York as a young actress; shipping magnate Aristotle Onassis's enormous $32 million yacht, *Christina*, complete with a seaplane attached, which Egypt's King Farouk had described as "the last word in opulence"; a guided tour of the living quarters of the Truman White House by the president and First Lady Bess, which included my little brother Douglas and me being taken to meet the First Lady's mother Margaret Elizabeth Gates Wallace, born in 1862! There was the visit to Salvador Dalí's home in Cadaqués, Spain; dinners at the Beverly Hills lavish homes of movie mogul Samuel Goldwyn and lyricist Ira Gershwin; or an afternoon on the Riviera with W. Somerset Maugham and

Noël Coward, for example. It was quite a life for my brothers and me.

My father was one of five children of a poor Romanian tailor who died when my father was eleven. His mother sold candy and individual cigarettes while he'd sleep below the counter on New York's Lower East Side. Whenever he'd take us to enchanting places and spend time with those larger-than-life people, he'd say: "Oh, Dad always took me to places like this." Or after an exciting night on the town with him, he'd gleefully ask: "Like the show so far?"

So that's how we came to know the Hemingways. A relationship between a newsworthy giant and a journalist soon evolved into an enduring friendship. We were never blasé about any of this. We just thought it was a normal upbringing.

II

THIS BOOK SINGLES OUT THE ONE PERSON WHO, BESIDES MY
father, and my wife Judy, has had the most profound and enduring influence on me: Ernest Hemingway. I met him when I
was seven. Just four years later, events he facilitated began to
unfold which would lead me to life-changing experiences that
still affect me. That's why I'm one of a dwindling number of
self-appointed keepers of the Hemingway flame. Nowadays, it
seems his great novels are no longer required reading in high
schools. Younger generations know his name, perhaps, but not
much about the incredible life he lived and his legacy of some
of the greatest works of the twentieth century.

There have been dozens of books about Hemingway, nearly
all of which were written by scholars who weren't lucky enough
to have met him and known Mary as I did, much less had a
long family relationship with him. One I recently read went
so far as to suggest he had contacts with agents of the NKVD,
the forerunner of the sinister Soviet KGB! Hoping to lure him
into their service, they reportedly even assigned the code name
"Argo" to him. But their plan supposedly never went anywhere.
I thought it was pure speculation, no more.

Hemingway was without a doubt a patriot. He was a
staunch anti-fascist who, like his friend and fellow author John
Dos Passos, drove an ambulance in World War I where he was
wounded with two hundred fragments of mortar. Like many of

the characters he created, Hemingway was often at the front lines of combat. During the Spanish Civil War, he was a correspondent for the North American Newspaper Alliance, a large newspaper syndicate. Although as a reporter he had to be ostensibly neutral in his dispatches, he was a fervent supporter of the Republican Loyalist side and later lamented the lack of support for the Loyalists from the US government.

By the time they first met in New York in 1937, my father had been writing "The Lyons Den" for three years. Slowly, the word had gotten around town to the usual haunts of the city's "newsworthy" people, that his was not just another tabloid gossip column. It was more important than that. He never revealed current romantic encounters, news of famous couples' "infanticipating" as his rival Walter Winchell put it, and such drivel. That was gossip fodder for other columnists. Indeed, years later, a journalism professor NYU made the column required reading for his students. In later years, other columnists filled space with several photos of "bathing beauties" and the like, whereas "The Lyons Den" usually had one photo of one of the luminaries written about that day, people from all walks of life, doing the things which made them newsworthy. He never used the word *celebrity*! "I'll write about my sister Rosie in Brooklyn if she's newsworthy," he'd say. And once in a while, my "*Tante*" Rosie was!

He worked from noon until 7:00 a.m., a grueling shift— hours which probably shortened his life, but he thrived on the daily challenge. Ironically, September 14, 2001, the day after his birthday, I calculated that I'd lived one day longer than my father. Ironic because that very day, I heard a report out of London that scientists discovered that we're basically supposed to sleep at night; that people working overnight shifts often die before their time. And so, he did—at just seventy in 1976.

Thornton Wilder, author of *The Bridge of San Luis Rey, The Matchmaker, Our Town,* and *The Skin of Our Teeth* among others, once said of my father's column: "If you write trivia, very often it turns out to be great literature." Although not formally schooled as a journalist, his background as an accountant and lawyer helped him keep his writing process to-the-point: clear, concise, and direct. In 2012, he was enshrined in the City College Hall of Fame, and when he retired in 1974, Mayor Lindsay gave him a medal at City Hall and Pete Hamill, the quintessential New York essayist and novelist devoted a full column in tribute to him in the *Post*. Not bad for the son of impoverished immigrants.

From 1939 to 1960, Hemingway's primary contact with important goings-on in New York were the columns my father would send every day. He read them when they arrived daily at Key West and later, starting in 1940, to Cuba. Hemingway referred to them as "The Clippings." Hemingway surely began to realize that he was frequently mentioned and must have enjoyed the friendship of at least one journalist who always got his facts straight. In fact, over the life of the "The Lyons Den," only FDR and Eleanor Roosevelt were mentioned more often.

The earliest stories about him to appear in the column came from Hemingway's time as a journalist covering the Spanish Civil War. One item from November 1937 reported that Hemingway took a respite from covering the front lines. Trying to relax in his Madrid hotel room, undeterred by bombs and artillery from Franco's Nationalists, he began moving the furniture around. The suite was arranged so that he could conduct what he dubbed "my indoor Olympics" using furniture as obstacles. What followed were races and other athletic tests in the room, a brief respite from the horrors of war outside. During a temporary time out from the "games" a friend asked him why he continued to stay at the Florida Hotel, where bombardments were raining down by the minute.

"You see," replied Hemingway, "this is the only hotel in Madrid with hot water. And besides, it's easier for a writer to get hot while you're on the lid of a steaming kettle."

After being wounded in World War I and surviving bombings all around his hotel in Madrid during the Spanish Civil War, he was almost killed again. It came in a London bombing during a blackout in 1944. He needed fifty-three stitches in his head. This was shortly after he'd come from New York and told my father he was headed to the front. He landed on the Normandy beaches on French soil as a member of the seventh wave on Omaha Beach on D-Day morning on assignment writing for *Collier's* magazine.

During the celebrations of liberation in Paris in late August, 1944, Hemingway introduced a woman to John Ringling North, co-owner of the circus known as "The Greatest Show on Earth. His brother Henry was a good friend. When the woman began sprouting the Communist Party line to North, Hemingway interrupted. "Forgive me, John," said Hemingway. "It's my fault. I had just introduced her to Picasso," who was a noted communist.

But this wasn't Hemingway's first foray into the war. Back in November 1942 and into the following year, he'd acted as a one-man navy off the coast of Cuba. Hemingway sailed his boat, the thirty-eight-foot *Pilar*, on many self-created missions scouring the blue waters of the Caribbean off Havana in search of U-boats which he'd heard were in the vicinity. Perhaps naively, he loaded his fishing boat with small arms, including a Thompson submachine gun, pistols, ammunition, and grenades, thinking he had a chance against a warship.

While certainly not a case of false bravado, his plan was well-intentioned but somewhat hare-brained and reckless. He was hoping to catch a German submarine at its most vulnerable point: recharging its batteries on the surface, a sitting duck, he thought. Hemingway foolishly surmised he could use his innocent-looking fishing boat to sneak up alongside a U-boat, typically 214 feet long, and quickly drop a grenade or two down its hatch before racing away. Some skeptics and Hemingway scholars suggest such forays were just an excuse to go drinking and fishing. But he really believed he might get lucky and help the war effort.

Luckily for the world, Hemingway never had such a dangerous encounter, for any U-boat would've surely spotted him approaching, aimed its large machine gun mounted on its deck, and blown him and all the novels and short stories he was yet to write out of the water! You can still see the *Pilar*, which has been restored and dry-docked, part of the tour at the Hemingway home, *La Finca Vigía*, outside Havana.

The relationship between Hemingway and my father had indeed been a friendship of opposites. Hemingway hunted big game on land and at sea and could be a boisterous hard drinker, sometimes even goaded into fistfights. My father, on the other hand, hunted anecdotes on the concrete "jungle" of Manhattan afternoons and evenings. The only "fights" my father ever engaged in were in print, hitting back at rivals like Winchell who'd always started it. He and Hemingway were opposites who were drawn to each other while spending dozens of evenings together at restaurants and nightclubs. It wasn't only the heyday of New York newspapers; dozens of nightclubs were flourishing, too. Nightspots like El Morocco with its famed zebra-skinned chairs and booths were jammed with patrons dressed to the nines. They frequented these swanky places as much to see as to be seen. There was the Copacabana, with star performers every night, and the posh Stork Club, Jack White's 18 Club, and Billy Reed's Little Club. The big sports bar and restaurant for lunch or dinner was Toots Shor's, with its Runyonesque owner sprouting gruff opinions on many subjects and greeting star athletes. Toots was the city's most colorful "saloon keeper," as he called himself, who in later years would often urge my three brothers and me to quit college and come work for him. One night my father brought an elderly Englishman on his rounds to the nightspots including Shor's. Toots, noticing he wasn't a retired athlete and had a British accent to boot, so he greeted the gentleman with a polite but disinterested "Hiya, Bub." Just then, in walked Baseball Hall of Fame member Mel Ott, the former New York Giants slugger. Shor spotted him and turned to the Englishman, saying: "Excuse me, Bub. Somebody important just walked in." Shor turned to greet Ott, leaving my father and "Bub"—Sir Alexander Fleming, discoverer of penicillin—because "somebody important" had just arrived.

III

Every night on the town in New York in that era was an adventure, and for Hemingway a welcome respite from the wars he covered as well as a sharp contrast to the perennial tranquility of his *finca* which fostered his writing.

Over the years, my parents were among the first to receive copies of his latest novel, with Hemingway eager to get my father's opinion. Looking back, I find that an unimaginable honor. It's as if Leonardo da Vinci had given a close friend a peek at *The Last Supper* before it was unveiled to the world and asked for his friend's opinion! Hemingway trusted my father, who in turn trusted Hemingway to give him exclusive stories about his doings. It was an unlikely but mutually beneficial friendship between a dapper, "street corner New Yorker," as my father proudly called himself, a Jewish lawyer-turned-journalist, and the large, robust Hemingway, a gruff Midwesterner, outdoorsman, big-game hunter, and fisherman who spent most of his life larger than Life itself. Surely thoughts about their strong friendship between my father and Hemingway flashed across my father's mind as he began to think of his farewell column to his old friend.

They'd met in 1937 at the Stork Club, which had already become a nightly stop on my father's rounds. The owner of the club was Sherman Billingsley, an Oklahoma-born former bootlegger during Prohibition. He constantly kept his eye on the door, making instant evaluations about arriving patrons. Then he would use a secret hand code to direct the maître d' as to where to seat arriving couples, according to their importance; the farther away from the kitchen (a table location he referred to as "Siberia") the more prominent the customer.

Billingsley was known for many things, but like his rival Toots Shor, not for being a voracious reader by any means. When for example, my father introduced him to Carl Sandburg, America's greatest Lincoln scholar, Billingsley said: "Next book you write about Lincoln, try and mention 'The Stork Club', will ya?" It was Billingsley who introduced my father and Hemingway.

By 1938, Hemingway had written a play called *The Fifth Column*. It opened on March 6, 1940, at the Alvin Theater on West 52nd Street. The cast included two stars. One was established: Franchot Tone, the suave leading man of that era who'd played opposite Clark Gable in the original movie version of *Mutiny on the Bounty*. The other was a rising young method actor named Lee J. Cobb, later to portray the lone holdout juror in *12 Angry Men*, the detective in *The Exorcist*, and nine years after the Hemingway play, created the famous role of Willy Loman in Arthur Miller's classic *Death of a Salesman* on Broadway.

The Fifth Column was directed by the legendary Lee Strasberg, the esteemed acting teacher, proponent of the Stanislavski "Method" of acting, whose wife Paula became Marilyn Monroe's acting coach and confidant. Hemingway based his play on a time and place he knew well: Madrid during the Spanish Civil War, which had ended just the year before. But despite his name on the theater marquee, a tepid review from the make-or-break *New York Times* theater critic Brooks Atkinson led to a disappointing run of only eighty-seven performances. It was an embarrassing flop. The play focused on two journalists holed up in Madrid while Franco's Nationalist forces were attacking the city, just as Hemingway and his future third wife, journalist Martha Gellhorn, had endured together. While he was at work trying to master the unique challenge of writing a play, the producer wired him in Cuba asking how far along he'd come with the script. Hemingway wired back: "It's finished. Now all I have to do is write the dialogue." But the different process of playwriting didn't suit Hemingway well, and he never wrote another stage play.

By 1940, Hemingway and my father had seen each other occasionally at the Stork Club and Shor's and realized that despite their vastly divergent backgrounds, they had some things in common which would forge a lasting friendship. Both were journalists, and both wrote only the truth: My father reported it, while Hemingway continually searched for it. His novels spoke of true values in characters he created. He gave my father a supreme compliment by sending him an early copy of one of his masterpieces: The first time came before the publication of his novel *For Whom the Bell Tolls* in 1940. The card accompanying the book in longhand read: "I hope you enjoy this. I liked your European pieces very much," a reference to some columns my father filed on what would be his last trip to Europe before the war. (On that trip to London, my father "accidentally" forgot to return the large room key at the Savoy Hotel. When he returned in 1945, they still had it in their records that he'd taken the key and assigned a bellboy to open his door every time he arrived.)

On rare occasions in those years, when traveling overseas, my father would write a reserve column or two with "evergreen" items while in transit. Those were timeless anecdotes about one person or a collection of anecdotes on one subject. It was necessary in the pre–jet era to spend a full day traveling, sometimes more if he went by ship. What's more, my parents would never fly on the same plane. My father often went on inaugural flights—airlines establishing new routes and inviting the press to cover it. My mother would go on the next flight. Many parents did that in those days when air travel was still considered a bit risky. Sometimes, in order to keep the columns as fresh as possible, he would ask friends to write a guest column while he was traveling. And not just any friends got the chance: Salvador Dalí, Jimmy Durante, the great screenwriter Ben Hecht, and photographer Margaret Bourke-White among them. (I've re-read the Dalí guest column several times and still can't make heads nor tails of it!) But when my father asked Hemingway to write a guest column, Hemingway would have none of it. He'd read those columns written by other friends and in a letter scoffed: "You can see why I didn't want to substitute for you if you read those columns."

While he took some time off from writing novels until the end of 1943, he'd been working on a technical book for the Army Corps of Engineers. Such was his fame as a novelist, however, that MGM executives heard about the project and expressed interest in acquiring the screen rights, sight unseen. "But this is a technical book," he protested. "We know," replied the studio executive, "but all we have to do is send a writer down to you and he'll fiction it up." It was not to be.

On July 14, 1943, the movie version of *For Whom the Bell Tolls* opened in New York at the vast Rivoli Theater on Broadway. Hemingway told my father he'd heard about an amazing example of luck outside the theater. A soldier had arrived at the box office that night, only to be told that the last tickets had been sold. As he walked away forlornly, a stranger nearby said: "I heard what just happened. Here's a ticket, Soldier." And that's how Pvt. Donald Friede, the former Hollywood agent, got in to see the opening night screening of *For Whom the Bell Tolls*, the movie he'd sold to Paramount for Hemingway, and for which he'd also represented the screenwriter Dudley Nichols and co-star Ingrid Bergman.

In early May 1944, Hemingway was poised to leave Cuba for New York en route to London to cover Operation Overlord, the invasion of Europe the following month. Before he left the *finca*, he had one more piece of business to attend to. He and his then-wife Martha Gellhorn had planned for the wedding of one of their employees at the *Finca Vigía*. A few days before the wedding, however, a young woman came by looking distraught. She told Hemingway that the groom-to-be was the father of the child she was about to bear. She was reconciled about his marrying someone else, but at least wanted to have a proper surname for the baby and wanted Hemingway to help her.

"If all you want is a name for your child," said Hemingway, "you may call it 'Hemingway.' Just be sure when you register the birth, you spell it 'Hemmingway' with two 'M's." And so, she did.

A few days before the landings in Normandy, Hemingway was in London, preparing to cover the historic event, the largest amphibious invasion in history. He was on assignment for *Collier's* magazine and had been assigned to the 4th Infantry Division. But a serious auto accident landed him in a hospital, unconscious. His injury to his head, while not life-threatening, nevertheless required fifty stitches. Soon after he regained consciousness, Hemingway heard the doctor asking him his name and occupation, to assess any loss of memory or cognition. It was then that he realized he couldn't speak clearly because of the cuts to his lip. He feared the doctor might think his unintelligible words were due to delirium. That would lead the doctor to order days of bed rest causing him to miss covering what would later be considered the most important day of the century. So, Hemingway decided to keep still for two days, then finally bellowed: "Let me up! I've got to get out of here in a hurry!"

Although he was in the seventh wave to land on Omaha Beach that day, Hemingway was at the front in some of the conflicts just after the landings. That's when he showed magnanimity toward wire service reporters. They were on tighter deadlines then he had for his magazine. So he gave the daily reporters information he'd gathered which he, as a magazine correspondent couldn't use. One of the correspondents was another famed author named Paul Gallico. He would later write *The Poseidon Adventure*, *The Snow Goose*, and other novels. Gallico marveled at Hemingway's ability to range far ahead of advancing troops on his own, oblivious to the danger. Gallico said, "At those times, it seemed that there was nothing standing between our side and the German Army—except for Ernest Hemingway."

In late July, 1944, Hemingway led a group of American troops and *Maquis* Resistance fighters trying to be the first to reach Paris for the city's liberation. Along the way, they reached a bridge still held by retreating German troops. Hemingway took charge, deployed his irregulars, and, following his instructions, they took the bridge. The pockets of resistance were finally crushed after house-to-house fighting. Then Hemingway teamed up with the novelist Meyer Levin (who eleven years later would write a "nonfiction novel" and the Broadway play and screenplay *Compulsion* about the Leopold-Loeb murders).

The two writers-turned-correspondents told the other journalists they were "going off to conduct research on any historical places in the vicinity." Two weeks later, their competitors, far behind, finally found their trail. On the walls of a liberated cathedral, the following words were scrawled: "Property of Ernest Hemingway."

Paris was liberated on August 19, 1944, but the war droned on. In December, German field marshal Gerd von Rundstedt's army made a breakthrough into American lines. Hemingway was still traveling with the 4th Infantry Division. By this time, they'd reached Luxembourg. This was during the Battle of the Bulge, which would be the last great conflict of the war in Europe. Despite enduring one of the coldest winters in history, Hemingway decided to shave his trademark bushy beard. As he would later relate to my father, an M.P. on the alert for Nazi spies masquerading as American soldiers spotted the author, drew his pistol and pointed it at Hemingway. Hemingway was wearing a yak-hide white winter coat, once worn by an officer in the *Wehrmacht —the German army*—on the Russian front, which made the M.P. suspicious. Then the M.P. asked for identification. Hemingway submitted his papers, but the photo had been taken while he still had his famous beard.

The puzzled M.P., who hadn't recognized Hemingway's name, studied the photo, which bore no resemblance to the now-clean-shaven correspondent. He studied the strange German officer's coat and finally said: "OK, proceed. No German spy would be so obvious."

In April 1945, Hemingway had returned to his other home, Key West. My father reported that a man named only "Stevens" showed up uninvited at his home and announced he'd heard so much about the author's ability with his fists.

He told friends he'd vowed to pick a fight with him. He said he'd trained rigorously for more than a year. So, he followed Hemingway to Sloppy Joe's, a frequent Hemingway haunt in Key West, and found the ideal way to provoke him. He saw Hemingway and one of his sisters leaving and addressed them in an insulting manner.

That did the trick of course. Hemingway began swinging and after several punches, "Stevens" tore Hemingway's expensive cashmere sweater which had just arrived from Abercrombie & Fitch in New York. "That does it!" said Hemingway and knocked the man out.

During the fall of 1948, my parents, for once flying together, had gone to Havana to visit Hemingway, but got their signals with him crossed. "We hit a hurricane off Hatteras" my father later wrote. That delayed their arrival by six hours and they never crossed paths on that visit. But it wasn't for lack of effort. After they arrived, a Cuban friend who knew Hemingway's haunts took my parents all around the old section of the city searching for him. "We went to a dance hall, a cemetery, at least 50 sightseeing spots, then hotels, but no Hemingway," my father wrote in his column. "We checked all the bars we knew Hemingway frequented including his favorite haunt *La Floridita* (which to this day remains a tourist mecca in Havana, with a life-sized bust of him at his favorite spot at the bar). That fishing trip you'd planned for us, Ernest, would've been wonderful," he continued, "even though my guts couldn't take it aboard the *Pilar*. But it would've been worth it."

Meanwhile, Hemingway was in fact doing the same thing that night: searching Havana for my parents. "Have just paged all the hotels and dragged all the bars," he wrote in a letter which arrived days later in New York. "No Lyons. Not even in a tea shop." It was a case of a teetotaler looking for a hard drinker while at the same time, the hard drinker was searching in tea houses.

Some years later, they had planned another reunion but once again, seemed to cross like two ships passing in the night. Literally. This time my parents were aboard a ship which was delayed en route to France and didn't have ship-to-shore phones. So, for two days, Hemingway waited for my parents in the lobby of his old haunt in Paris, the Ritz Hotel. He had little to do. Then the hotel manager noticed Hemingway sitting in the lobby looking bored. He reminded him of the old steamer trunk he'd stored in the hotel's basement. It was put there when Hemingway was en route to cover the Spanish Civil War in 1937.

Hemingway had forgotten about that trunk, so he suddenly had *plenty* to do! He spent the next two days going over the contents of the trunk, which proved to be a treasure trove of literary history. The items included his rough draft and notes for his novel *A Moveable Feast*. Oddly, Hemingway's manuscript spelled it "Movable," and his editors at Scribner's decided to leave it that way, without the "e." It would be published posthumously in 1964. His fourth wife Mary had it published with the "e" restored and sent the first copy off the presses to my parents. It was a memoir of his youth in Paris while married to his first wife, Hadley Richardson. Hemingway rarely made notes in his working copies. "If it's good, it's engraved on my mind," he explained to my father. "If it's not good it erases itself."

A short but sad note from Hemingway came in a letter which arrived in December 1945. It was written in longhand, and mentioned the recent death of humorist, critic, columnist, and actor Robert Benchley, one of the wittiest raconteurs of his time. "Still feel awfully bad about Mr. Benchley," he wrote. "It will never be the same town to me without him. The kids [Hemingway's three sons] feel terribly too."

A letter from Hemingway arrived in July 1949, in which he talked candidly about his health. "I'm dead pooped," he wrote. "I try to get good exercise, so I'll sleep and be ready to hit it [his writing] again."

Soon after that, he wrote about an injury he'd suffered in yet another accident, explaining that it happened

offshore near the finca. *"I was recuperating from a fall I took on the flying bridge of* Pilar. *It was a very heavy sea and the deck was wet. We were coming in to anchor and I was going to relieve Gregorio [Fuentes, his Spanish-born captain, first mate, and longtime fishing companion] at the wheel so he could anchor. He swung* Pilar *broadside to go through the reefs just as I had my good leg over the rail. My head hit one of the clamps which hold the hooks of the big gaffs in. Although I braced myself with my shoulders and took most of it there and hung on to the rail, I got the real straight up fireworks. It amounted to a five-inch cut that reached my skull and severed the artery and gave me a con-cussion. Mary and a friend got the hemorrhage contained OK and we got to a surgeon in about 5 hours. Somehow, they avoided it from being just another Tragedy of New York Society Sherman's and Toots' society.*

Mary won the prize for the largest marlin taken in the International Tournament here, fishing from Mary's own boat the Tim Kid. *It was the smallest craft entered and represented the Ketchum, Idaho Rod and Gun Club.*

Best to you as always, Lenny and to Sylvia and the boys, Ernest.

IV

IN THE EARLY FALL OF 1950, HEMINGWAY WAS COMING OFF some negative reviews for *Across the River and Into the Trees,* which had earlier been serialized in *Cosmopolitan* magazine. He was now at work on a new novel. By then, he had been living in Cuba, first in Havana at the downtown hotel *Ambos Mundos* (which today has a huge display of large photos of him on the walls of its lobby along with a giant reproduction of his signature, plus a commemorative plaque outside). He and his third wife Martha Gellhorn began living there in a small room in 1940 (room #511, now a museum) before she found a small farm forty minutes outside the city. For just $12,500 ($224,315 in today's dollars) they'd purchased the *Finca Vigía,* half an hour or so outside the city. It was built in 1886 by a Spanish architect, a Catalan named Miguel Pascual y Baguer. The rooms were sunny, designed to be cooled by the tropical breezes. It was there that he would write his most important novel, *The Old Man and the Sea* in 1951, the last work of fiction published during his lifetime. It would win the 1953 Pulitzer Prize for Fiction and lead to his being awarded the Nobel Prize in Literature the following year. The proclamation for that prize read in part: "For his mastery in the art of narrative and for the influence that he has exerted on contemporary style." It would be made into a memorable 1958 film with Spencer Tracy and later a TV version with Anthony Quinn which aired in 1990. When we returned to the *finca* twice in 2017, the curator proudly showed us the Nobel Prize which sits atop his desk in his library. Some one thousand books adorn the shelves. Others were falling victim to years of humidity and were transferred to the Kennedy Library. They total more than nine thousand and many have his notations in the margins.

My father let him know how eager my parents were to read what would be his most famous novel, so on September 8, 1950, Hemingway wrote:

> *Dear Lenny,*
> *You'll get your book, pal. Only I have to get it first to sign it.*
> *Be a good patient boy and I hope you and Sylvia like it. It's*
> *BETTER THAN ANYBODY KNOWS. (that's a secret,*
> *but if you don't like it pan it.) Thanks for Jim's address.*
> *[Jimmy Cannon, one of America's greatest sportswriters*
> *from the* New York Post, *my father's flagship paper, had*
> *been a correspondent in World War II.]*

The night the news report that Hemingway had been awarded the Nobel Prize reached Cannon's usual table at Toots Shor's, Cannon stood up, sighed, and announced: "Excuse me, everyone. I'm going home to beat up my typewriter."

In that same letter, Hemingway went on to express his dislike of Clare Boothe Luce, the flamboyant wife of Time-Life founder and chairman Henry Luce. She was a famous woman in her day, a former actress who'd understudied Mary Pickford on Broadway when she was just ten in *A Good Little Devil.* Luce also wrote several Broadway plays including *The Women* as well as its screenplay and stories for the movies *Come to the Stable* and *The Opposite Sex.* Later Luce was elected to Congress in 1943 and served as a conservative Republican from Connecticut for two terms. In 1953, she was appointed Eisenhower's ambassador to Italy, a rare post for a woman at that time.

Despite her impressive resumé, Hemingway had little regard for Luce's sense of privilege. Writing about the nearly three-month-long Battle of the Hurtgen Forest, which lasted from September 1944 to February 10, 1945, Hemingway wrote of his son Jack being wounded in the fighting. Clare Boothe Luce was there as a correspondent for *Life*, her husband's magazine (reportedly created based on her idea). "I didn't like the looks of this Clare very much because she looked like she had a rebuilt nose or something and her hair wasn't the right color for her age," he wrote. "She was the guest of the transport command or some sort of rear echelon thing." Then he took particular exception to the fact that of all the women the troops would've seen in a long time, the first one had to be Luce, then forty-one. On the other hand, closer to the front, Hemingway wrote that "once in a long time I would catch a glimpse of Marlene [Dietrich, who he adored] which always gladdened my heart."

No wonder. There was a party at our home in 1950 honoring Ethel Barrymore, where Hemingway and Dietrich were among the guests. Years later, my father recalled that he'd noticed Hemingway and the sultry Dietrich were spending the evening in a corner of our living room in an intense conversation. By that time, I was old enough to understand what a "your-place-or-mine" chat was about.

After that party, my father saw Dietrich during his nightly rounds and she recalled that during that evening, she told Hemingway she was dating a man who occasionally got rough with her. When he heard that, Hemingway stood up, grabbed her arms, taught her how to turn sideways, cover her face, then quickly throw a left hook. Sometime later, he heard she'd learned her lesson well. When her date got rough, she threw that punch, landing a direct hit on his chin on what was, no doubt, their last evening together.

Hemingway continued on about Luce in the letter.

Well, this Congresswoman in the soldier suit came over and started to tell us about war. It seems that either the Transport Command or the Quartermaster's were everything. War is truly gigantic and we were microcosms. So, one of the characters who was looking at her admiringly but not hearing so good said: "Did you call me a god-damn microscope, Ma'am? I'm an infantryman! I am not a 'microscope.'" So, this Connecticut woman with her diamond rings explains that he was in no sense a "microscope" but a microcosm; that what she wanted us all to know and appreciate was the vastness of the effort (she had been well briefed) and that we were the tiniest pinpoints at the end of this vast and heroic effort in which every American, and I presume especially the voters of, say Connecticut, played their just and assigned parts.

You could clearly feel his disgust with her.

At this, another of the characters began gazing at the congresswoman admiringly, and perhaps a trifle hungrily as my Black Dog looks at the appearance of a sizzling steak even if you know it is not a first-class steak though it is. I guess if you can chew it and swallow it you would probably be nourished thereby. Best to Sylvia and the infield, Ernie.

One night at the Stork Club, my father sat with Hemingway, who began talking about his craft. "I write for a living," he explained. "I'm not an 'artist.'" Although years later a tour guide at his home in Key West told us Hemingway wrote everything in pencil, this was untrue. He also used the same battered old typewriter and said of it: "It needs cleaning badly but I'm like a baseball player who hates to change his uniform when he's on a hitting streak."

The descriptive titles of his books were important to him, as they are to every author. "I want them to be poetic and mysterious," he said. *For Whom the Bell Tolls* is a perfect example.

With one glaring reservation, he was pleased with the movie version, which he'd seen in eight installments in theaters around the world. He didn't like the love scene. On another night at the Stork Club he told Ingrid Bergman, who starred with Gary Cooper in the film, why their love scene didn't ring true.

"He didn't take his coat off," said Hemingway of his pal Cooper's portrayal. Cooper portrayed Robert Jordan, the American volunteer fighting with the doomed Republicans in the Spanish Civil War. "That's a helluva way for a guy to make love, with his coat on."

Hemingway's letters to my father were very different from his published works in style and could be quite revealing. They spoke to the essence of the man and were free from the constraints of telling a long, involved story. He trusted my father as he trusted very few friends. His candid letters revealed some of the substance of the man behind the legend. For example, he said: "I can write a letter easily, but it's almost always indiscreet. That's because I loosen up as completely as I can. I lost my facility in writing when I started to break up my own writing and rebuilt it like architecture."

He was a man of his times. Hunting elephants, rhinos, and lions in Africa—unthinkable to most people nowadays—didn't have the moral and environmental taboos it carries today. Some contemporary critics will say he was chauvinistic, but that was then, this is now. In Havana one night, to that point, he gestured to a lady seated at a nearby table wearing a bulging sack dress and shook his head. "A woman's gown ought to have a reason for being," he said. "It ought to make a woman look desirable." Different times.

My father wrote of his friend: "Hemingway was what we call 'a two-fisted drinker.' I saw him flatten a pestering man one night, too, but for that he needed only one fist. But I've also seen him in his moments of tenderness. It was at his home outside Havana. I'd brought my three older sons there. Our eldest, George, who was then fourteen, asked: 'Mr. Hemingway, how do you write a novel? Do you make it up?'

"'Yes,' replied the greatest novelist of the twentieth century, 'you make it up. You invent it. You make it up out of everything you've ever known, from all the things you've ever seen and felt and learned. You imagine it, from day-to-day, and then write it down, as if you're telling the story yourself or to your children. That's how you write a novel.' Then he added: 'And you pretend the words are being tattooed on your back. That will keep your sentences short and to the point.'" Sounds simple.

He said he wrote "with the feeling that this will be a book which won't have a single word changed," from the way he would write if it were the last and only thing he would ever write.

When Hemingway was back in New York for a visit in 1948, he shared his table at the Stork Club with my father, which by now had become a ritual between the friends. Their talk turned to Hemingway's reputation for getting into fights in bars. But he brushed it off. "Down in Key West, everyone has at least three or four fights a day," he said, "and we just call that 'ordinary exercise.'" Again, different times.

One prevailing quality throughout all the letters from Hemingway was a sense of honesty and even occasional self-deprecation. For example, in March 1945, he was introduced to a *Life* magazine writer named George Frazier, who told him that while at Harvard, he'd won a medal for a thesis he wrote about Hemingway.

"It's still in the files at Harvard, so if you're ever there and . . ." Hemingway interrupted him and said: "I couldn't get into Harvard. I never went to school. I never had enough credits to get into any college, especially Harvard."

"The Lyons Den" column reported that for nearly a decade Hemingway had a lumpy scar in the middle of his forehead. It was an unwanted memento of a long ago fight in which he suffered a cut that had been stitched hastily and carelessly. After he survived car crashes in England and Havana, the old scar was finally removed. In the Havana accident in early August 1945, he crushed the steering wheel with his chest. Later that day, he went to his frequent watering hole, *La Floridita*, where he was asked about the mishap. "I broke my steering wheel and it'll take three weeks to replace it," was his only explanation of the accident.

September 1945 brought news of an eventful fishing trip Hemingway made with his oldest son Jack, who in later life would also become a world-class angler. Also aboard the *Pilar* (by then retired from Hemingway's fruitless anti–U-boat forays) was a professional jai-alai player. Jai-alai is a Basque game, sort of a much faster version of handball played with a curved oversized straw claw called a *cesta*. The ball is thus whipped against a wall at incredible speeds. It's played on an enclosed handball-like court. Jai-alai is no longer played in Cuba but was popular back then. In fact, when we visited the Hemingways in 1952, he took me to an indoor stadium to watch a game. You could make bets on the game as it progressed by writing down numbers of some sort on a carved-out tennis ball, which he let me toss back down near the court.

That day on the boat, Hemingway hooked a large marlin. Anticipating a prolonged battle to reel in the huge fish, Hemingway strapped himself into his fishing chair and told the athlete to stay below, lest he accidentally interfere with the lines from the reel. Several hours later, as the exhaustive battle with the huge brave fish was nearing its end, the jai-alai player had had enough of lying below decks. So, against Hemingway's orders, he opened the door to the top deck and got tangled in the lines, which forced Hemingway to cut the exhausted marlin loose and dejectedly watch it swim away. Then the embarrassed jai-alai player cried out: "Toss me overboard. I no longer deserve to live!"

A letter we received from Hemingway in 1949 gave more insight into his writing process. He was discussing the importance for any writer of word counts. Somehow, decades before today's word processors, Hemingway had the uncanny knack of knowing the count of the words in his newest book. He took "three days off for my birthday and have hit this week with 552 on Monday and 805 on Tuesday. 687 today," he wrote. "These are words. Let's hope all deathless ones. I hit that tower [at the *finca* where he did much of his writing] in the morning and when I get through, I'm dead pooped. Then I try and get good exercise so will sleep and be ready to hit it again. Get a secretary out twice a week to clean up my business."

The year 1950 brought the novel *Across the River and Into the Trees*, which he said was not the original title. He'd intended to call it *Over the Water and Into the Trees*, but he changed it, since he thought it wasn't up to his standards of being mysterious and poetic. It didn't help since the book, which had previously been serialized in *Collier's* magazine, got mixed reviews and is one of his lesser works. (Various filmmakers, from his friend director John Huston to Burt Lancaster and director Robert Aldrich, had tried to make it. Now, finally, it is being produced with Liev Schreiber in the starring role. It's about a former Army Colonel, haunted by his wartime experiences, living in post-war Venice. Giancarlo Giannini is set to costar.)

Early in February 1950, Hemingway sent my father a copy of a letter he'd written to the *Sunday Graphic*, a British tabloid. It was in response to their review of *Across the River and Into the Trees*. The *Graphic*'s critic had given a scathing review of the novel, even going as far as calling the book "evil." What's more, he even suggested: "Mr. Hemingway deserves to be hanged. You may spare yourself any legal embarrassment," he wrote.

Hemingway's response began by telling my father he'd suggested "shipping the author of the article and your book editor over here to the above address [the *finca*]. Then they can give me satisfaction at the conventional distance of ten paces and I will ship them both back to you if you want them. We will give them a good rest; feed them well and provide them with two friends if they do not bring any. I will feed them, however, only for two nights and a day. I look forward to seeing these gentlemen tremendously and I regret that their stay here will be so short, although I hope that it will be instructive." The letter was addressed to the paper on "Fleet Street or thereabouts."

However much satisfaction that letter brought him, Hemingway was surely mollified by the subsequent review of his book in the *Sunday Times* of London, a much more prestigious publication. It was written by another great American writer, John O'Hara, whose popular novels included *Ten North Frederick*, *Butterfield 8*, and *From the Terrace*. O'Hara called the book "the loftiest piece of prose committed to paper since 1616," the year Shakespeare died. Unlike even Hemingway, O'Hara was that rare writer so respected that he never permitted one word to be altered by an editor. But he made an exception this time when he allowed the *Times* editor to insert that Hemingway was the "outstanding author since the death of Shakespeare."

The over-the-top denunciation of *Across the River and Into the Trees* in the *Sunday Graphic* had little effect on sales, however. Scribner's ordered twenty-five thousand extra copies printed on the day of publication, a total of one hundred seventy-five thousand, while the London publisher sold thirty thousand copies even before publication! After attempts to film it by no less than directors John Huston, and Robert Altman and by the star Burt Lancaster, Pierce Brosnan is slated to star in a version currently in preproduction. Not bad for a book which got mixed reviews seven decades earlier!

In late March 1950, my father printed a quote from Hemingway in which the novelist boasted that he proudly held the title of "The Worst Dressed Man in the World." That prompted an immediate response from Russel Crouse, who adapted the legendary Broadway hit *Life with Father* and produced *The Sound of Music*, among many others. Crouse sent a telegram to my father at the Stork Club reading: "WHERE DOES ERNIE HEMMINGWAY [*sic*] GET OFF CLAIMING THE TITLE OF 'WORST

DRESSED MAN' WHICH I HAVE HELD . . . ?
WHEN THERE IS A NEW WRINKLE IN CLOTHES
YOU CAN ALWAYS FIND IT IN MINE."

My father then mailed the telegram to Hemingway in Cuba who wrote across the bottom in print: "I CHALLENGE YOU, CROUSE. I WILL DEFEND YOU WITHOUT MERCY. YOUR OLD COLLEAGUE, IMPLACABLE ENEMY ON THIS TERRAIN, ERNIE." He then mailed it back to us, and my father passed it on to Crouse.

Later that month, Hemingway wrote: "Hope you and Sylvia and your infield [my three brothers and me] are fine. Mary broke her leg in two places, skiing like a damned champion at Cortina [Italy which would be the site of the 1956 Winter Olympics]. Last year it was the right leg. This year the left. They had some 420 broken legs at Cortina. I have the first draft of the new novel all corrected and will get proofs by the first of May. Scribner's plan to publish again. Going to be very busy with the publisher here, so will have to skip the joints [i.e., nightclubs] this time. We had good duck and goose shooting and Venice and Paris were both as fine as ever. Am a boy with five hometowns now: Paris, Venice, Ketchum, Idaho, Key West and Havana. No aspersions on other towns. Best always, Ernie."

Nevertheless, even though he never owned a home in New York, Hemingway couldn't keep away from one of his favorite cities for very long. The next month he was back in town and entered the Stork Club with a scraggly beard and tweeds and as if to solidify his hold on that dubious title, again proclaimed: "I was voted 'The World's Worst Dressed Man' and I'm here to defend my title!" It was his last night in town and he said he'd vowed not to visit the nightclubs on this visit but confessed; "I tried but couldn't go the route."

He had fond memories of the Stork Club. Soon after he sold the film rights to Paramount Pictures for *For Whom the Bell Tolls*, he'd celebrated there. When he sent for the bill, Hemingway used his $150,000 check he'd just received and asked for change. Proprietor Sherman Billingsley was unfazed: "It's only midnight. If you wait until closing time, we should have enough in the till," he said, casually. When Hemingway returned to the nightclub, he reminisced about that story, telling Billingsley: "When I sell the movie rights to my new novel, I'll again bring the check. Only this time, you'd better have change for $300,000!"

Then in early April 1950, a handwritten letter arrived from the *finca*, lamenting the fact that Jimmy Cannon was taken off the sports beat by the *New York Post*, to cover the Korean War. "Sure hate to see him off sports and on that. It's like seeing a friend go back on the junk. I mean it makes you feel so sad." He was a Hemingway pal from frequent visits to Toots Shor's restaurant. Hemingway admired Cannon and his writing concise writing style enormously. Occasionally, Cannon wrote a "Nobody Asked Me" column with wry observations on life.

"Imagine having to go to war when you can't take a drink," Hemingway continued in that letter. " But Jimmy didn't drink anything at the last one, either as I recall. Well, I guess if I live to be a hundred or so, they would say I died of drink like my great grandfather at eighty-six and it was a shame I'd had a misspent life just hitting that bottle."

"Have no intention of mixing in this one unless it spreads to Europe where I speak the language and could do some good. Meantime we Hemingsteins [*sic*] HAVE Jack a Capt. of Infantry in Berlin and my kid brother Leicester is going in. There is plenty of time on this one. War gets to be a pain in the ass when

34

you've been going to them since you were eighteen years old. After the last one, I thought my kids wouldn't have to go to any more. They always give you that crap and you pout and do all you can. Then they say: 'That was all just in a manner of speaking. Come on, boys. We've got a new one. Just suited to you.'"

Hemingway claimed he'd set a style of short hair for men. He liked that. His heroine years before in *For Whom the Bell Tolls*, played by Ingrid Bergman, had cut her hair short. Before returning to Havana, he was in the Stork Club again where he said: "If I die, I'd like to die quickly and be a beautiful corpse, but now it's too late."

He left New York disappointed because his friend Henry Ringling North had refused to allow Hemingway to work with the lions and tigers at the Ringling Bros. Circus. He wrote: "Henry's refusal to let me work with the big cats saddened me, but I had hoped he'd let me do something constructive with the rhinoceros." (Did the circus ever have a rhino?)

Back in New York soon after that, Hemingway lunched with my father and told him that before breakfast every morning, he'd lie on his back, then sit up without bending his knees. Then he'd do it again ninety-nine times more to toughen his stomach. Part of his morning ritual was weighing himself on an old doctor's scale. Then he'd scribble his weight on the wall of the bathroom. The scale and scribbles on the wall remain to this day, one of the stops on the tour of the home, where tourists, prohibited from entering the home, can peer in and check his weight.

"Hit me in my stomach," he said. Reluctantly my father arose and complied. Hemingway just laughed, while my father massaged his bruised wrist.

At about that time, Hemingway cofounded an imaginary club for heroes only, and which he called simply "The Club." In a letter from early April 1950, he explained:

> *It was founded by Henry Ringling North, Mike Burke and myself. [Burke had been an OSS agent during the war, then an executive at the Ringling Bros. Circus, and later, with CBS, ran the New York Yankees before the team was sold to George Steinbrenner, and the Knicks and Rangers before they were sold to the Dolan family.]*
>
> *We were the only members of "The Club," except for one canine member, named "Chickee." He was supposed to bring "The Word," an engrossed parchment containing some form of citation for alleged heroism. At the command: "Chickee! Fetch 'The Word,'" the dog would come back holding the parchment to give to any member present. That member would then be briefed immediately and take off on some extremely hazardous mission.*

The imaginary "Club" would eventually have seventeen members and a mythical elephant courtesy of North's circus, trained to lop off the heads of any applicant deemed unworthy of membership, or so North claimed.

In May 1950, Paul Gallico returned to France to visit the places where he and the other war correspondents had stayed. He asked the hotel owner if any of the other journalists had made the sentimental journey back. "Only one," said the man. "The bearded one—M'sieur Hemingway."

Then came a cablegram from Havana dated September 1, 1950:

DEAR LENNIE PLEASE KILL THE LETTER ABOUT CLAIR [sic] *AND NEITHER USE NOR SHOW ANY OF IT STOP THEY APOLOGIZED FOR COVERAGE AND WHY BOOT SOMETHING LIKE THAT WHEN YOU ARE WINNING STOP WILL WRITE SOMETHING ELSE FOR YOU SOME- TIME STOP SCRIBNERS ORDERED ANOTHER 25,000 PRINTED THE DAY IT CAME OUT MAK- ING ONE SEVEN FIVE WITHOUT BOOK CLUBS WHICH NEVER SUBMITTED STOP IN LONDON SOLD THIRTY THOUSAND BEFORE PUBLICA- TION. [Scribner's] HAS PRINTED THIRTY MORE AND IS ORDERING MORE PAPER STOP GOOD LUCK PAPA.*

(I suppose I'm violating a request from Hemingway by including his remarks about Amb. Luce earlier, but my father never published it in the column and by now they belong to posterity.)

About this time, my father arranged for Rocky Marciano to visit Hemingway at the *finca*. "The Rock from Brockton, Mass," as he was affectionally called, would retire as the undefeated heavyweight champion in 1956 winning forty-nine bouts with forty-three knockouts. He was so eager to meet Hemingway, Marciano arrived earlier than expected. Outside the home there still stands a bell which visiting guests would ring (today a favorite stunt and photo op for tourists) and the Champ duly rang it loudly. Thus Marciano was greeted a minute or so later by his host, who was wearing shorts and was bare-chested. Marciano said: "You're in great shape." Hemingway replied: "I wasn't showing off, Champ. If I'd expected you this early, I'd have worn a shirt, tie and jacket."

February 1951 brought several letters from Hemingway, sent from the *finca*. "I am not writing a musical for Josephine Baker [the great chanteuse of that era] or anyone else," one letter began. "I've had all sorts of propositions submitted and so far, have accepted none. My job is to write; then when I come to town [New York] I can have some fun. What I've actually done is write 25,000 words of as good prose as I know how to write from Jan. 12 to Feb. 15. This town is full of displaced gamblers. I ran into a boy I hadn't seen in about thirty years, and he said: 'Is it true, Ernie, that you've gone straight and are writing books in stiff covers?,'" the favorite Hemingway description of his works.

February 2, 1951, brought one of the longer letters from Hemingway, also written at the *finca*:

> *I am sorry that have been so busy that I haven't written you, but I thought your cable took care of the letter and I have really been working like hell on the long book [*The Old Man and the Sea, *which eventually turned out to be a short novel.]*
>
> *Lenny, what goes on in that town? A fellow named Condon came out here and said he was a partner of José Ferrer and wanted me to write a forty-page story of a musical with Ferrer and Gloria Swanson. I told him to save his time. The answer is "no." He kept on talking and talking and I tried to explain to him I was writing a serious book and could not interrupt it. Finally, he got up to sums like 150 and 250 G's and I thought he acted sort of like a mental case. Don't quote me on that. But he was sweating and talking and poured himself two glasses of Holland's gin and water and gulped it down. To get him out of the house, I gave him Al Rice, my lawyer's address, and told him if he*

had any concrete propositions to submit them to Rice and Rice would submit them to me. The next thing I read is that he has signed me to do a musical for Josephine Baker.

Henry Wallace who works for either UP [United Press] or AP called me up to confirm the story and I denied it exactly as I have to you. I am not writing a musical for Josephine Baker or anyone else. Nor will I. Nor have I.

This Hy Gardner [a competing columnist for the New York Herald Tribune *who'd written an erroneous item about Hemingway] writes that Josephine is considering my musical. Also, that the last time he mentioned me (in a faked item) I wrote you to punch his nose for me.*

The nose business I don't mind except that I have never hit a newspaper man in my life, nor I hope, been rude to one. I was in it too long and know what it is. Am interested in the propositions to televise the stories but all of that has to be cleared through Rice, my lawyer. Also, movie deals, etc. My job is to write. Then when I come to town, they can have fun.

Give our best to Sylvia and your ball team. Mary gets back this afternoon. She took our Venetian house guests for a slight tour of Florida and the Gulf Coast before they had to go back to Europe. . . . Jack is still in Berlin and is going to have another baby. He writes the doctors say this time it will be a boy. I know you are not an obstetrical columnist but I knew you were fond of Jack and thought you'd like to know. Best Always, Mister Papa.

Jack would have two daughters: the late Margaux and Mariel, both successful actresses. He once jokingly lamented: "I'm the son of a famous man and the father of famous daughters."

V

On March 3, 1951, "The Lyons Den" informed its readers that a young writer, who'd had some measure of success with his first work, met Hemingway and spoke of the future of novel-writing. "Suppose I'm lucky enough to turn out a best-seller and sell it to the movies for a big price," the young writer began. "But in these days of high income taxes, so little of it would be left to me. What do you suggest?" "Learn now, and write later," Hemingway advised.

On June 29, 1951, Hemingway's mother Grace Hall Hemingway died. She'd been an opera singer, taught music, and was a painter. A few weeks later, he wrote again, almost as if nothing had happened. "I hope you and Sylvia and the boys are all well. Mary gets home tonight at midnight from visiting her family and a trip to Upper Michigan and Minnesota. She had cool weather, so it was good luck. Really hot here at the *finca* now.

"Best to you always, Lenny. I haven't forgotten about the book. It is such a bloody nuisance to get it through Customs here and then get a permit to send it north (wartime regulations still in force) that I hoped you wouldn't mind waiting until I got to New York for it. Excuse dull note. Am working very hard, Ernest."

Most of Hemingway's letters to my father were typed, but others were handwritten. One such letter was dated October

6, 1951, sent from the *finca*. My father had wanted his friends William and Grace Boyd to visit the Hemingways. A longtime movie actor, William Boyd had begun in silent films back in 1918, made the leap to "talkies," then television. He became one of early TV's biggest stars, the black-clad hero known to a generation of young fans (including this one) as "Hopalong Cassidy" and for many years, he led the Macy's Thanksgiving parade astride his famous white horse named "Topper." But their meeting with Hemingway was not to be; the letter read:

> *Thanks for you note of October 2nd, would have been delighted to entertain your friends the Boyds but because of Pauline's death [his second wife Pauline Pfeiffer who had died six days earlier in Los Angeles], we were not making any engagements. Am sure both you and they will understand. When they are here another time we will get together.*
> *Hope everything goes well with you and all of yours,*
> *Best always, Papa.*

At that time he was hard at work, consumed by making finishing touches on *The Old Man and the Sea*. He wrote: "Right now, I am concentrated [*sic*] on trying to get a book out which will not have one word changed from the way I would write if it were the last and only thing I would ever write and everything that I have found out about life is in it. With luck in getting it published properly, it will be read by more people than ever."

In early January 1952, my parents, my three brothers, and our grandmother and I were vacationing at the Grossinger Pancoast Hotel in Miami, owned and operated by the family which ran the most revered of all the famous Catskills resorts. That's where the invitation came from Havana to come visit the Hemingways. Havana, then a haven for American tourists and with casinos run by American mobsters, was the capital of a country under the harsh rule of dictator Fulgencio Batista. It would be seven years later that Fidel Castro's army, part of his "26th of July" movement overthrew the tyrant.

My younger brother Douglas sensed something special was up. He wanted to go along to Cuba too. But at just four and a half, he was deemed too young to make the short flight over to Havana on a rickety DC-3 via Cubana Airlines. "I won't touch anything!" he pleaded to no avail. (Today, as a senior New York Legal Aid defense counsel, I'm sure his skills at pleading his case have vastly improved.) Thus, to his everlasting regret, he was left behind with his grandmother and I still kid him about it to this day!

My father devoted a full column on January 7 to that visit, which I remember vividly.

> *"Papa" said Mary, blond and radiant, "tell the cook to put twice as much chicken in the Arroz Con Pollo." (The staple of many dishes in Spain.)*
>
> *When Mary telephoned to invite us, she forgot to ask the ages of my sons and thought they would be older. "So twice as much chicken, Papa," for she knows the appetites of youngsters are lustier.*
>
> *My sons, who address me as "Papa" had not been told that all of Ernest Hemingway's friends call him "Papa" too. That compounded the confusion which often arises when several boys arrive. At the lunch table, Hemingway began to answer the questions my sons addressed to me.*
>
> *Hemingway is at work revising his new novel, now exactly 283,251 words long. [It would be* Islands in the Stream, *published posthumously in 1970 and adapted into a*

movie with George C. Scott as a Hemingway-like character.]
"I've lived like a monk these past two years" he told us,
"seeing few people, just writing." He showed us the trunk
where his manuscript is stored. In case of fire, the house-
hold staff have been instructed first to save "The Bank"
as he calls the trunk. Then they were instructed to save a
Miró painting, probably the best of the Spanish surrealist's
works. Hemingway had bought it from the painter in 1922
when they were both poor in Paris. Now, when he ships it
to museums for exhibitions, the insurance premium is ten
times as much as its original cost. "But first the trunk with
the book," Hemingway repeated. [That painting would
be the subject of a prolonged custody dispute and has been
gone from its place on the wall in the dining room for years.
The custodians of the finca told us they still expect it to be
returned someday.]
He showed my sons his hunting rifles and the mounted
heads of some of the animals he's shot. One was the Cape
buffalo and my 11-year-old son Warren asked: "Were you
afraid?" Papa nodded. He showed the boys the skull of a lion
he'd shot and once more Warren asked: "Were you afraid?".
He then invited the boys to accompany him to the field and
shoot. George was reluctant and said he couldn't shoot well
enough. "You can with me," Papa said.

I remember Hemingway telling me that they'd recently had trouble "with some bandits" in the area, so, since I was still in the latter stages of longing to be like the pistol-packing cowboys I'd seen on TV, I was thrilled at the chance to shoot a real gun. (Different times. I outgrew my childhood fascination with guns decades ago.) "You come with me," he beckoned. "A *real* pro will never make you look bad."

"We followed him into the field alongside the house and the tower he used to write. There on the cement steps of an abandoned hut, the houseman had set up an assortment of opaque empty liquor and wine bottles of several colors as targets."

I remember asking Hemingway how he got so many nice bottles.

"Hemingway smiled," my father continued. He loaded the .22 rifle, then showed my fourteen-year-old brother George how to hold it. "The boy fired and missed. 'You've got to shoot as if it's going to kill you if you don't kill it,' Papa told him." George fired again and the bottle smashed dead center. Then my second son, Warren, took the gun and Papa showed him how to aim.

> *Warren seemed nervous and Hemingway talked to him softly; "You've got to get calm first, calm inside, as if you're in a church when that lion's coming toward you. You get calm inside and you've got something to believe in. Then shoot the sonofabitch!"*
>
> *Then he sat down, so that his height would be level with Jeff's [that's me] and circled the boy's shoulders to help him hold the gun. They fired a round, and the boys went off to the swimming pool. Then Mary and Papa took turns with the gun, and then smashing of the bottle targets sounded like the night Dutch Schultz, the gangster, was cornered and escaped. We joined the children at the pool, and I told them of the first time I'd met Papa, 16 years ago, when he'd invited a group of us to punch his hard stomach. Howard Hawks, the great director of movies like "The Big Sleep," "Red River," and "To Have and Have Not," once broke his wrist punching Papa's stomach. Hemingway invited the children to punch him and it was like corrugated steel.*

Sylvia tried it too. "Papa," she told him, "it feels as if you wear a girdle tighter than mine."

"Boys," Papa told them, "you got to keep your stomach muscles relaxed in a fight but hard for a surprise blow." Then we returned to the living room where Hemingway pointed to his work sheets which he burns after the novel is completed. The manuscripts will go to the New York Public Library. But not his work sheets. "The finished book is the skin of the animals," he said. "People don't care about seeing the meat and the bones." My boys now looked at him with awe and affection, for though they were too young to have read his books, they knew they were in the presence of greatness.

Hemingway spoke of his own sons, who recently came into an inheritance. He's trying to take care of their property, but the legal work is getting too much for him. "By the time I get through writing one of those legal letters, I could've written a short story which would be easier for me to do," he explained.

Dusk was settling over the finca, and across the valley we could see the lights of Havana being turned on. Ernest and Mary accompanied us down the path in front of the main house and Papa stopped at the ancient Ceiba tree to pluck an orchid for Sylvia. And we said goodbye and drove back to the city, now plastered with Batista's new campaign signs touting his latest fixed election: "Este Es El Hombre" they proclaimed. I translated it for my sons: "This Is The Man" and they asked me: "Who? Papa Hemingway?" "Yes, Papa Hemingway" I replied.

I'm the only person still alive who was there that unforgettable afternoon, and I would return to the *finca* twice in a space of six months—sixty-four years later! More on that visit later.

Soon after that indelible day, my father printed a news item about Hemingway, surely obtained while my brothers and I were cavorting in their swimming pool—the pool where Ava Gardner had swum naked. (That's how tour guides describe the pool.) He reported that although some of the foremost universities in America asked for the original manuscripts of his novels, he decided to donate them to the New York Public Library. "If the purpose of such collections is to have young writers learn from them," he explained, "then the manuscripts should be in a place which is really available." He felt that a young writer shouldn't have to make a trip to Princeton or Cambridge to study a manuscript. "And besides, New York is the city where I feel most at home."

This was not to be. The New York Public Library, guarded by the large concrete lions "Patience" and "Fortitude" (so named by then-Mayor La Guardia as qualities New Yorkers would need to survive the Depression), had limited space. After Hemingway died, the Castro regime allowed Mary to return to Cuba and sort through his papers after she'd obtained special permission for the trip from President Kennedy. What she took out of the *finca* was put on a shrimp boat headed to Tampa. The cargo included papers and paintings, but many of his papers and artifacts including his Nobel Prize medallion are still at *La Finca Vigía.*

There were other papers dating back to 1935 which Mary found in 1962, only these were in an unlikely place. Incredibly, they'd fallen behind the bar at Sloppy Joe's in Key West, one of several Hemingway drinking haunts. These Key West papers— lying untouched for more than a quarter of a century—were infested with rat skeletons but thankfully some survived. Others were found in the basement of the Ritz Hotel in Paris where he'd often stayed. Most of the papers found are now in the John F. Kennedy Library in Cambridge, Massachusetts, perhaps as a thank-you to the president for granting Mary that travel exemption from the Cuban blockade. The collection at the library was dedicated in 1980 by Jacqueline Kennedy Onassis and Patrick Hemingway, the second of his three sons.

Sometime after our visit to the *finca*, when he was back at his usual haunts in New York, Hemingway told my father he writes three versions of a novel. He burns most of the earlier versions. "Why should anybody be interested in the mistakes I've made?" he explained to my father. "The writing in the finished version is the best I know how to do." He said he wrote the first version in longhand or at a typewriter placed on a shelf chest high and often worked standing up. The rewriting for the second and third versions was done while he was seated at a desk. "Dictating is not for me," he said. "I could dictate a novella a month if I had to, but it wouldn't be good enough."

Soon after my family's visit to the *finca* in early January 1952, Mary Hemingway wrote my mother:

Dear Wonderful Sylvia,
What a remarkable woman you are to run that mob so well, to take such first-class pix and then to remember that we love to have them, especially because they remind us not only how photogenic but also how flourishing the personalities are in your outfit.

Since you left, things have quieted down. My battle of the tomatoes is like a World War. You win it but then right quick you lose it. After a disastrous defeat last year, I won this year over Gardner's Indolence, Tomato Hornworms, Springtime Enervation and assorted leaf-eaters. So, what have we got? The house is overrun with tomatoes, friends and neighbors graciously declining further baskets, red, ripe and juicy and beautiful.] The Deep freeze is loaded with juices and sauces and purees, all tomato. What a pity the cats don't eat them, or that I can't send you a couple of bushels. This comes under Country Life.

Papa and I, alone with the two boatmen, took a ten-day fishing trip which was absolute heaven—wonderful fishing with no telephone or mail, complete silence and the stars at night. And cool enough for me to sleep in my skiing underwear, which down here, is great.

Dear Sylvia, thank you, very much and best love to you and your team. Why can't you do it (i.e., come down) more often?

Mary

Late in January 1952, Hemingway's hometown, Oak Park, a Chicago suburb, was anxious to hold a day in his honor. Part of the planned ceremonies would be the display of his old high school football uniform and cleats. But Hemingway thought the honor was undeserved. "I barely made the squad," he recalled. "I was probably the worst football player they ever had!"

In February 1952, he was invited to join a Sportsmen's Club, but living in Cuba, he would not be allowed to join. A local American embassy official in Havana heard about it and told Hemingway—possibly as a joke—that if he joined, he would have to surrender his passport. Incredulous, Hemingway asked: "Would you really want to make me a man without a country? That'd be pretty hard, especially considering that my ancestors were Cheyenne Indians."

Later that month a cordial letter from him arrived, beginning with an apology:

Dear Lenny, I felt terribly not to have written after you wrote such a fine column after that good visit we had with Sylvia and you and the kids. I feel bad too not to have written to thank you for trouble you took to send the columns.

The reason I didn't write, kid, was because I avoided writing any letters that were fun and no trouble and cracked down on everything I had to do and didn't want to, or had put off, to get squared away to take a vacation. Mary and I wanted to go down the coast in the Pilar where there would be no telegrams nor bad news nor problems and take a rest. Planned to stay all month if possible and I was going to write you from the boat. Took a writing board on the boat and some envelopes and paper along. We had a wonderful trip for a week. Then Mary went in with Gregorio, my mate, to get some ice at a little port named La Mulatta. She called the house to see if things were okay. That was how we learned poor Charlie Scribner had died on the same day we had left Havana harbor." [Charles Scribner was his longtime publisher.]

So, we are back at the Finca now. I was terribly fond of Charlie and feel like hell that he is dead. Am no good at writing about people when they are dead although by now, I should have learned how to do it. But I guess it is one of those things you can do or not.

Anyway, you take care of yourself. You looked in wonderful shape when you were down here and so did Sylvia. It was lots of fun to meet the boys and finally have you out at the place.

Excuse this for being sort of a gloomy note, Lenny. It is the first letter I've written since we got back last night and

I don't look forward to the ones I have to write now.
Caught some wonderful fish and wish you were here to
eat them with us.
Mary sends her very best to you all. [Handwritten:]
So do I.

Like all famous people, Hemingway hated lies or mis-statements often written about or attributed to him. On April 15, 1952, for instance, he sent my father a letter which took a swipe at Hemingway's old friend Sidney Franklin, the Jewish, Brooklyn-born bullfighter, the son of Russian immigrants. Franklin became the first American to be confirmed as a full matador in *Las Ventas*, Madrid's venerable *Plaza de Toros*, the most important bullring in the world. It's been called "the Carnegie Hall of bullfighting" and the crowd is traditionally austere, the most difficult to please.

Hemingway and Franklin had known each other for some three decades. They'd met in 1929 during a great epoch in Spanish bullfighting. In *Death in the Afternoon*, Hemingway's classic 1932 scholarly book on bullfighting, he'd praised Franklin's work with the large magenta and yellow cape called the *capote*, as well as his bravery and style. Franklin had been an occasional companion when Hemingway was covering the Spanish Civil War, even visiting some of the front lines with him, since he too was a correspondent for the Newspaper Alliance of North America. They'd been close friends who'd shared danger together.

In 1952, Franklin published his memoir, *Bullfighter from Brooklyn*, about the unlikeliest path anyone ever took to an arena in Spain. Late in the book, Franklin disparaged some of the other journalists who, like Hemingway, were covering the bloody civil war. Franklin claimed "some famous correspondents" had been writing their prejudiced stories from the safety of Paris, then filing them from Spain to get a Madrid dateline, as if they'd been near or at the scenes of combat all along. "It made me hate their guts," he wrote. "I never could have believed that such world-famous writers would trade their names so cheaply and stoop so low."

That prompted this from Hemingway to my father:

I don't know whether you've been reading the pieces from Sidney Franklin's autobiography (serialized) in Vanity Fair. To put it mildly, he remembers many things a little differently than I do. But in the last article, he says some things about the correspondents in Madrid during the Civil War that I must protest against. I never knew a group of newspapermen who worked harder and more courageously under almost impossible conditions than the correspondents in Madrid and I want to protest against what Sidney wrote about my colleagues.

Lenny, you know that I cannot write and correct every misstatement made about me. Instead of being a novelist, I could get a full-time job as a misstatement-corrector. But I hope there will never be a time when I will not write to correct a misstatement made about my friends, I have admiration for the way all of them behaved in that difficult and dangerous time. I protest most strongly at what Sidney wrote about them. If a writer thinks fiction is necessary in his autobiography, then I think it would be simpler if he put the fiction in italics. Best regards, Papa.

VI

THE SEPTEMBER 1, 1952 ISSUE OF *LIFE* MAGAZINE FEATURED A somber-faced Hemingway on the cover and inside the entire text of *The Old Man and the Sea*. Think of it: The same day the book hit the bookstores, you could read it for a mere twenty cents, the price of a copy back then! Inconceivable today. (I recently bought a copy in near mint condition for $2, but eBay was selling them for $100!)

In October 1952, with the book already a bestseller, Hemingway was awarded a medal by the government of Cuba. *The Old Man and the Sea* had sparked tourism to the island beyond the gambling crowd. It would solidify him as the foremost American novelist of the century. He accepted the medal on behalf of his fellow fishermen: "those in the little boats who go after the big marlin." The Hemingways invited all the fishermen and their wives from the nearby village to attend the presentation ceremonies. When it was over, the medal Hemingway received had to be returned because it bore the stamp of the pre-Batista tourist commissioner, and a new one had to be struck for the occasion.

May 22, 1952, brought another letter in which Hemingway, still peeved, continued his attack on sometime friend Sidney Franklin. "Thank you very much for publishing the correction I had to make where Sidney was speaking so badly of the newspapermen in Madrid," he wrote. "When I thought of all the good friends I had there and what a libel it was on them, I had to make a correction and you were very kind to publish it. The last thing I want to do is interfere with Sidney making a living. And if I corrected everything he wrote, it would interfere with his livelihood."

When my father again asked Hemingway to write a guest column, he replied: "I don't think it would be a good idea for me to write a column for you about all the crap that has been printed about me because it would make enemies and if your policy is not to squawk, then certainly you should not squawk in bulk. As for exciting things or dangerous things they always sound like bragging. Lenny, I lost my facility in writing when I started to try to break down writing and rebuild it like architecture. I can write a letter easily, but it is almost always indiscreet because I loosen up as completely as I can."

Then, a glimmer of hope. "But you tell me when you need the stuff and I will try like hell to do it even though I write for a living and have not the time nor money to take the vacation I have wanted to take in Europe for two years. But this fall, Mary and I are going to try to get over there. You know I have not even been to town for two years."

He then, alas, reiterated his strong reluctance to write a guest column. "I'll let you have three shots at me at ten paces rather than write a column for you. You do it so well and so easily it must seem silly to think how impossible it would be for someone who has disciplined themselves into the kind of damn writing I try to do.

"If you needed it to keep out of jail, or if you were broke, or owed money and were in trouble, or if you or Sylvia were ill, I would be glad to write your column as well as I could and fill in for you. I would come to town and stay up all night and not drink and move around and write as good a column as I could if you needed me to. But if I write a bastard half-assed column for you down here which would have nothing but my name to recommend it, then my name would not be worth much for long."

In November of that year, the world premiere of the movie version of his 1936 short story "The Snows of Kilimanjaro" was to be held in Havana, so he could attend. The movie starred Gregory Peck, Ava Gardner, and Susan Hayward. But Fox studio head Darryl Zanuck called it off. The government press protested, reminding the movie mogul that the press and Hemingway were planning to attend. "Exactly," replied Zanuck, "and Hemingway might tell all the reporters he doesn't like what they've done to his story."

On May 4, 1953, Hemingway won the coveted Pulitzer Prize for Fiction for *The Old Man and the Sea*. The very next day, he wrote my father. "We had a wonderful trip down the coast and listened to the newscast in a big squall, really big one, just when we heard about the prize. Then the Cuban radio had it on the air every fifteen minutes for a couple of days. But you can always shut off the radio. Imagine if you would ask me what my reactions were, and I had said a lot of people including myself would've been happier if Native Dancer had won the Derby. But I am going to watch my Goddamn mouth now for a couple of years and see what happens. Maybe I will get respectable. Wouldn't that be wonderful?" (Native Dancer, the favorite in the 1953 Kentucky Derby, was the first racehorse made famous via television but suffered the only loss of his career to Dark Star.)

Hemingway sent his Pulitzer Prize check to his eldest son, Jack, a paratrooper stationed at Fort Bragg, North Carolina. "It is the same as five months' jump-pay," said Hemingway. "My best to the mob and love to you all, Papa."

On June 25, 1953, my father spent a remarkable day in New York with Hemingway. Remember, these were different times; big-game hunting today has largely become an anachronism —endangered species need to multiply, not be killed. But back then, it was a different story. The whole idea of "endangered species" didn't exist. Hemingway, almost as famous for his exploits as a big-game hunter and fisherman as he was for his novels, invited my father to go elephant "hunting" in Manhattan, which my father wrote about the next day:

> *I can say I went elephant hunting with Ernest Hemingway. But the truth is they were not real elephants, only paper targets and our African "plain" was a Madison Avenue shooting range. The gun was real, and the only casualty was a Lyons: Me! Let's start from the beginning.*
>
> *We had breakfast at Leland Hayward's apartment, which the Hemingways were occupying. [Hayward was the five-times-married producer of memorable films like* The Old Man and the Sea, Mr. Roberts, The Spirit of St. Louis, *and* The Sound of Music.*] The manuscript of Hemingway's new novel was in a bank vault in Havana, and they were leaving for Africa the next day in search of elephants. Not to shoot them. "I don't like to kill animals," said the man we all call "Papa." His wife, Mary, will photograph them and Papa will stand behind her with his heavy elephant gun, in case the beast should charge.*
>
> *Hemingway had some old .577 shells he wanted to test. We went to Abercrombie & Fitch, the famous sporting goods and clothing store. He carried the ammo and I the gun. "If it's heavy, you're out of condition," he said. "When it's light,*

*you're in shape," he said. He spoke of an offer from a mag-
azine to write a novel on order, for much money, but he
rejected it. "You can't write a novel to order," he said. "You
write it because you must, whether you can sell it or not."*

*A salesman led us to the basement and opened the door.
It looked like a cement telephone booth. He opened a small
metal door, like a safe and it led to a long shooting range.
"I was here last with Winston Guest," said Papa. [Guest,
nicknamed "Wolfie" by Hemingway, was the wealthy
Anglo-American polo player, lawyer, and horse breeder and
related to Sir Winston Churchill. He was an old Hemingway friend.]*

*"He was trying out his harpoon gun. He fired it only
once and lost a finger." Hemingway cleaned his eyeglasses.
"Bad eyes," he said. "Your eyesight gets burned from the rays
off the sea." He loaded the large double-barreled gun. The
shells are big ones. He once had hunted in Africa with Alfred
Gwynne Vanderbilt, Jr. [the extremely wealthy sportsman]
who brought only 10 of those .577 shells and said: "I didn't
bring more because they cost so much." [A .577 shotgun shell
nicknamed the "Nitro Express" is an enormous shell, about
the size of a salami. It has a velocity of 1,860 feet per second and a very heavy recoil. Hemingway's sixteen-pound
one-of-a-kind shotgun had been manufactured in 1913
and was previously owned by the aforementioned Winston
Guest. In 2011, it sold at auction for $340,000.]*

*Hemingway braced himself and fired. The salesman
covered his ears against the blast. "You don't fire until it's
20 feet away," Papa said about the elephant. "Shoot lions at
one hundred yards in 3¾ seconds. You've got to break bone.
If you gut-shoot a lion, it won't stop him. You've got to shoot
like a surgeon to break bone."*

He gave me the big gun and warned me to brace myself against the recoil. I did and aimed and fired. Nothing happened. A dud. "Better it happened here, than in Africa," said Hemingway. Then it was time to fire the second barrel. This time I forgot to brace myself and as I fired, I was slammed against the concrete wall behind me as the gun fell from my hand. "You okay?" the salesman asked. I suffered only a wrenched shoulder. "Lucky," he said. "They usually break a collar bone." Hemingway laughed. "Believe me, the animal would feel worse."

We went upstairs. On the train from Key West to New York he had sneezed and his belt burst. He bought a new one, 40 waist. "Used to be 48 chest, 38 waist" he said. He also bought a pistol. "Good around camp for small game, and intruders" he explained. He spoke of deep-sea fishing: "Watch the boat vibration. If you can hear it then the fish can hear it too and won't come up. That's the only trick."

We walked to the Guaranty Trust Bank, to put his trust accounts in order. "Never yet sold a share of stock I bought," he said. "Never had to. I can ride out any depression as long as they put me in a chair and give me pen and paper." When all the banks closed in '33, he had withdrawn $30,000 and kept the cash in his pocket "to discipline myself." He offered money to the poet and witty critic Dorothy Parker and the humorist and actor Robert Benchley, but they laughed at him and didn't think the money was real.

Hemingway then signed his income tax checks. "That estimated tax business," he complained. "How can any writer estimate his sales?" he wondered. He began to sign traveler's checks and said of his long name "I was overnamed." His signature, different from his book dedication writing was designed to make forgery difficult.

We lunched at Shor's and Toots said of his Old Man and the Sea, *"Great book. I read it. And if I can read it, anybody can." Toots told of the hand-kissing lesson Papa once gave him: "Simple. You take their hand like this, but don't throw 'em off balance." Toots also told the story of Hemingway and Hugh Casey, the late Brooklyn Dodger pitcher, trading blows while standing in an open doorway in Havana. A knockdown every punch. Papa won. He never even lost a tooth. "Spitting teeth is for suckers," he said. [Ironically, both men in that fight would die by their own hand and both used shotguns. Casey took his own life almost exactly ten years to the day before Hemingway died.]*

"In shooting, you got to be careful," Hemingway then said. "Not worried. There's a great difference between being careful and being worried. Take the cockroach. He goes to the kitchen, eats and doesn't worry."

Dinner was at the Colony; dining with us were the Haywards and Spencer Tracy, who will play the "Old Man" in the movie. They'd taken Tracy to meet the fisherman in Cuba, who accepted him without knowing he was a movie star. "Mary and I had so much fun, it's almost as if we're sinful," he said. We got into a cab and he told the driver "Sutton Place South" [one of the most upscale parts of New York]. Then he spoke some words in Italian to the driver. "You an Italian boy?" the driver asked, and said he came from north of Venice. "Then what are you doing on Sutton Place South?"

"Doin' good," replied Ernest Hemingway. "Doin' pretty good."

During that visit to New York, he paid a return visit to George Brown's gym, where the owner attested to the speed of Hemingway's left hook, the one emulated by Marlene Dietrich. He then received an inquiry from the British *Who's Who* publication, inquiring about his education. Hemingway had written that he'd attended public school, but in England "public schools" are what we call "private schools" or today's "independent schools." So, the editors accepted a compromise when Hemingway said "Kindergarten."

He returned to Spain and in early July to Pamplona, the sleepy northern city which comes alive for one week with the celebrated *Féria de San Fermín*, made world famous by Hemingway's *The Sun Also Rises*. Today, there is a larger-than-life bust of him not far from the *Calle Estafeta*, the street where the six bulls and several *cabestros*, the "Judas steers" run, headed to the corrals behind the *Plaza de Toros*, the bullring. (They're called "Judas Steers" because they lead the bulls to their imminent death later that afternoon.) Think of Mardi Gras ten times over, for no one gets much sleep for a week. In the main square, diners and drinkers move from one restaurant to another, as each one reaches its closing time. There are bullfights every day with the top matadors driving up to the small city to perform. Today, women can finally join the men in the running of the bulls, or in Spanish, the *encierro*. The men wear white pants and T-shirts, a red bandana, and many carry a *bota*, a goatskin pouch containing wine. It's consumed frequently by holding the *bota* aloft and swallowing the stream between your front teeth.

Later, dangerous and speedy cows of the breed race into the arena, their horns covered with boxing gloves, as the sleep-deprived runners stagger around and try to do passes with small capes or newspapers before many of them are knocked down.

"It was 30 years ago since I first went to Pamplona," Hemingway wrote us on July 11, 1953, from a *pueblo* about thirty kilometers outside the city: "It's still a hell of a fiesta; up at 4:30 in the morning, turn in at 2:30 the next morning. So, excuse such a short note.

"Thanks for looking after me so well in town. Wish we'd had more time. Best always, Papa."

On another visit to New York, he shared a table with my father at the Stork Club where my father thought he noticed a decoration in Hemingway's lapel. It turned out be a small rip in the buttonhole. "I never wear decorations," Hemingway said. "I didn't wear decorations, even during the war. They can't force you to wear medals. You can't be disciplined for it, even if the invitation reads 'Decorations will be worn.'"

The next time we heard from Hemingway wasn't until late January the following year, 1954. But first came some terrible news. They were in East Africa that month on a photo shoot. As a Christmas present for Mary, he'd chartered a sightseeing flight when word flashed around the world that he and Mary been killed in a small plane crash. But there was more news. Incredibly, it was the second crash of the day! Earlier, they'd walked away from the first mishap in a single-engine Cessna near the Murchison Falls in a remote part of Uganda when the pilot was trying to make an emergency landing. Hemingway suffered multiple injuries to his spine, shoulder, arm, and left leg, and a concussion. Also damaged were his liver, spleen, and kidney, and he temporarily lost vision in his left eye. They were spotted by a BOAC pilot and rescued by a tourist launch which took them to a place called Butiaba, on the shores of Lake Albert.

Just two days later, a second small plane, this time a de Haviland Rapide, picked them up but then that plane crashed and burned on takeoff! Somehow, all aboard escaped, although

Hemingway suffered more injuries. Back in New York, my father was on a deadline when the awful news came. He began his column thinking they had perished, as most other newspaper reports did, though he wasn't entirely certain. So, his tribute column began: "If it should be true," he wrote, "I'd bet he was calm in the face of this violent end." He recalled Hemingway's advice to my oldest brother George at the *finca* before George fired his rifle. "You've got to be calm inside, as if you're in church and you have something to believe in," he'd advised the boy. "He always has sought the places of violence," my father continued, "wars, the fight arenas, the bullrings. 'It's always easier to get hot while you're on the lid of a steaming kettle' he'd said. He was the Champ and he knew it, the way all champions do. He spawned a school of imitators, and plagiarizers. One imitator in particular irked him. 'He'd steal 'em as soon as I'd write 'em. I found a way to stop him, though. I stopped writing for two years—and he starved.'"

"He once pondered getting a tattoo. It was when he led the race to liberate Paris in 1944. Hemingway was decorated for this feat and when some jealous other writers suggested that he'd gone way beyond the non-combatant limitations of an objective war correspondent, Hemingway said: 'From now on, I'm going to have the Geneva Convention rules tattooed on my seat, with the words printed backwards so I can read them in a mirror.' There was ample proof that he was first at the combat regions. When the American troops finally reached the Cathedral of St. Michel, they found a sign reading 'Property of Ernest Hemingway.' Marlene Dietrich once said: 'Papa is more than a man. He is a way of life.'"

John O'Hara, one of the few writers able to be mentioned in the same sentence as Hemingway, and who was so eloquent when news came of Hemingway's actual death, once insisted to Hemingway that no man was strong enough to be able to break a shillelagh, an Irish walking stick. Hemingway accepted the challenge, found a shillelagh, and snapped it over his own head.

"His constant travels for new experiences led to the fuller life which helped enrich his talents. Before he left New York to cover the war, he told his lawyer: 'I have a great new novel.' When the lawyer asked where the manuscript was, Hemingway, pointing to his head, said: 'In here.'"

"As an aspiring journalist, he tried to land a job on a Chicago newspaper, but the city editor refused to hire him. 'He was right,' Hemingway recalled years later. 'He'd asked me if I knew where all the police precincts in the city were located and I didn't.'

"The *Toronto Star* did hire him, however, and assigned him to cover Prime Minister David Lloyd George's visit to New York in 1923. Hemingway followed the P.M. to the Music Box Theater where, inside, the Sinn Fein faction of the I.R.A. had bought a large block of tickets. As soon as George sat down, the protesters arose and began a loud demonstration against him. But the Star didn't have that story the next day. That's because young Hemingway, believing Lloyd George was safe for three hours at a Broadway show, went off to attend the Charlie White–Pat Moran fight. He was fired, just as his friend Orson Welles was fired from his job as a reporter for skipping out of an opera the night an understudy went on at the last minute. "When he returned home from World War II, Hemingway's language at dinner tables in New York was surprisingly polite, considering he'd just come back from near the front," my father wrote. "'I used up all the dirty words in the war' Hemingway explained. He once was invited to dine with

W. Somerset Maugham [author of, among others, *The Razor's Edge*] and Erich Maria Remarque [author of *All Quiet on the Western Front*] and brought along a young aspiring writer. 'I brought him along because I thought it would be good for him,' Hemingway explained, 'in case he ever writes his memoirs.'

"He once told me why he prefers to shoot wild fowl instead of clay pigeons. 'Did you ever try to eat a clay pigeon?' And on another occasion, he told me: 'If I die, I'd like to die quickly and be a beautiful corpse.'"

As he was finishing his column late that night, good news suddenly arrived: "My office has just phoned with the happy news that the Hemingways are alive. Every writer will please step back a bit, for the void has not yet opened at the top."

It wasn't until two weeks later, February 11, 1954, that we heard from the recuperating Hemingway. The letter was sent from New Stanley Hotel, Nairobi, Kenya Colony. "Dear Lenny, Thanks very much for the piece. I did not deserve it and will try not to make it necessary for you to try to beat it. Mary is fine. Tried the .577 (shells) to make certain they weren't blanks and were very useful weapons. All the solids were O.K. as we checked them out." Later, Hemingway took great delight reading some of his obituaries in dozens of newspapers from around the world.

In May 1954, Hemingway was in Venice and encountered longtime newsreel narrator Ed Herlihy. He introduced himself to Hemingway and said he still felt badly about prematurely announcing the Hemingways' death on NBC radio. "Oh, that's OK," replied Hemingway. "I saved you the cost of flowers. But I'll settle for a drink."

August brought a two-page handwritten single-spaced letter, written in the Gritti Palace hotel in Venice.

*Hope you, Sylvia and the kids are well. If that Look maga-
zine piece came out [detailing their plane crashes] you have
our news, more or less. Miss Mary is fine now. Her ribs
OK. She was banged worse than she knew but she is very
brave and has the guts of a badger.*

*After a proper examination they found I bought it
pretty thoroughly. Full concussion—loss of sight of left eye.
Optic nerve is regenerating OK. Loss of hearing left ear,
ruptured right kidney, ditto liver and spleen, intestines col-
lapsed, paralysis of spleen, etc. Couldn't shit for 22 days then
had 62 movements (complete with cramps in 20 hours all
standing up. If I sit down my lower intestine comes out.
Running as an indestructible can be a tough trade). So will
skip the atrocities. But tell the boys nothing is bad if you say
to it "go fuck yourself."*

*Sure could have used you to joke with. Lenny, you get
very fond of your friends when you are up Short Creek.
I tried to show that in the (magazine) piece. Well, after
I get the piece off (my pilot) and I land on a beach with
the Cessna. This is a little showboat but a little big good
too. So, what happens? It is very dry again and a brush
fire starts right behind the camp and will burn out a place
where there are a lot of kids, etc. So, we have to turn it and
try to canalize it. So, I get 2nd degree burns on legs, abdo-
men, chest and mouth. Got 3rd degree burns on left hand
and right forearm.*

*Patrick was shoved back to Tanganyika. Young Denis,
my partner, has attack of amoebic dysentery and can't move.
Miss Mary is crazy as a goat but doesn't know it. It is a
magnificent situation. So, Miss Mary takes the safari to*

Mombasa. At this time, she is in her watch-buying epoch and gives a watch to every game scout and gun bearer that is worth more than they make in a year. They are all in love with her anyway and she doesn't have to give watches. Watches are the smallest things she can think of. She starts with Omegas and goes through the Rolex Oyster perpetuals.

Shit-warm, Lenny. It was like old times in town. I bring the chartered boat back. I steer my watch OK and bring her in to the old anchorage at Fort Jesus, Kenya (very easy) and stay four days. Africa excellent and feast-good food. It is very pleasant in the old harbor. Never thought we'd make Venice but made it OK. All wounds healed good and sound.

Here there exists always certain problems. Fine, beautiful lovely problems. Tomorrow we go to the country. Then off to Paris to pick up a couple of clothes and bet 6 horses. Then to Spain to try to get in shape. Very good RAF doctor told me I could leave in 2 months if I kept my mind on it. Could live 2 years if I made it a career. We figure to beat him by ten. But lost so much blood, internal, that must keep pace myself and so we'll ship [to] New York and come straight home. Tell Toots and the mob that I will come quiet. I don't want to see some jerk like Billy Rose [the millionaire producer, showman, and lyricist] when I still have a concussion. The objects now are Paris, Madrid, Santiago de Compostela [in northern Spain, were there is a famous religious pilgrimage] and the Finca and Black Dog [his famous dog "Negrita" which I remember and who is buried at the finca]. Best to the family. Read this letter to Toots, would you mind? Or to Sherm, too. [Sherman Billingsley, Shor's bitter rival.] Fuck 21 and all their Colonels [a reference to another more sedate restaurant.] Best always, Papa.

October 9, 1954, brought another letter which Hemingway had written from the *finca*:

Dear Lenny, Thanks ever so much for sending the columns and also the Saturday Evening Post *piece about why you didn't want your boy to marry an actress. [Ironically, nine years later, my father arranged a blind date for me at the University of Pennsylvania with a classmate, a lovely California girl he described as "probably shy, being all alone so far from home. Her parents are old friends of ours." I remember being skeptical and reluctant but decided to do my father a favor and called this "shy," probably homesick girl: Candice Bergen, who surely never tells that story about me.]*

Mine are all married, so that problem doesn't arise. Hope you and your family are all fine. Give my love to Sylvia. I suppose if you had a girl, you wouldn't want her to marry an outfielder. This is just a note, Kid. I have been very remiss about writing because I have been trying to work very hard and people kept interrupting with visits and so forth. Now have had to make a hard and fast rule and I'm not going to see anyone under the circumstances until the first of March. Have finally got into writing well again and the back and the rest of it is all coming along good.

It seems such a long time since we had so much fun in town together. I would have loved to come back through town but knew I shouldn't as I was working hard getting my insides in shape and that is not the place for it. I'm glad you had fun in Venice, if you did. It sounded pretty overrun with people from the column.

As you know, Kid, I will always be happy to see you if you come down here to the finca. It is always fun and I always learn a lot. But let the word out if you feel like it that I am working hard on a book of stories and seeing nobody, repeat nobody. Honest to God, Lenny, this is the only way to get my work done.

If this note sounds particularly stupid it is because I worked hard all morning and we have what looks as though it could be a bad hurricane coming up and that makes problems for any character with a farm and a boat. [Hemingway was referring to Hurricane Hazel, the deadliest hurricane of the 1954 season. A category 4 hurricane, it killed 469 people, mostly in Haiti and later the Carolinas on October 15th. Cuba was spared much of its wrath.] One on a hill and the other in the water. Best always, Papa

On October 28, 1954, Ernest Miller Hemingway was awarded the Nobel Prize in Literature after the publication and success of *The Old Man and the Sea*. But the Nobel Prize is given for a body of work as well. He thus joined Sinclair Lewis in 1930, Eugene O'Neill six years later, Pearl S. Buck in 1938, and William Faulkner in 1949 as the first Americans to win the prize for literature. John Steinbeck would win it in 1962.

In announcing the Nobel Prize being awarded to Hemingway, the Swedish Academy said in the citation: "For his powerful, style-forming mastery of the art of modern narration." The day before the official announcement, the *finca* was besieged by newspapermen who wanted a statement from Hemingway. The dispatches from Stockholm stated the choice had been narrowed to the American writer and to Halldór Kiljan Laxness of Iceland, who would win the following year. "What can I say?" Hemingway told an insistent correspondent from Sweden. "At this time, all I can say is that I stand ready to offer my congratulations to Mr. Laxness."

Once the announcement became official, the cable desk at the local post office in the tiny *pueblo* San Francisco de Paula near the *finca* was swamped with congratulatory messages from all over the world. One from Ingrid Bergman read: "THE SWEDES AREN'T SO DUMB AFTER ALL." The sole operator on duty sat at a small wooden desk with one telegraph key and one typewriter, working without relief for extra hours. Cables reached Havana in a short time as well, and the main office there could have forwarded the avalanche of cables by bus within an hour. But this was (and still is) Cuba; rules were rules and had to be followed to the letter. The messages went by wire to San Francisco de Paula's office. It took four days to deliver them all.

In his acceptance of the award, Hemingway was magnanimous, saying it should have gone to Carl Sandburg, which was an unprecedented sentiment for a recipient. Sandburg—America's greatest Lincoln scholar—would win the Pulitzer Prize but somehow never the Nobel honor. He'd heard about that remark and said: "Thirty years from now, some bright young man, sitting around, will ask his friends: 'Say, did Carl Sandburg ever win the Nobel Prize?' and some *brighter* young man will say: 'Yes, Ernest Hemingway gave it to him back in 1954.'"

In late December, Hemingway cabled my father saying he was already hard at work on his next book. As for winning the Nobel Prize, he said: "No matter how valuable a prize is, it may do you more harm than good if you let it. No prize is worth interrupting work writing a good book."

Then a letter dated December 17, 1954, arrived, written aboard the *Pilar*. "We have gone down the coast to get away from the place and to be able to get some rest and work. I just got your wire and your letter down here when a bunch of mail came down. You know how I always enjoy seeing you and hearing about things in general. You have been one of my true grand friends for a long time. Also, we've had a lot of fun together."

But then he expressed some animus toward another writer: "What's happened to John O'Hara, Lenny or is he just more like himself than ever? Maybe he couldn't forgive me from walking away from those aircraft and not taking his advice on how to win that Swedish prize by breaking off with all my old friends, etc. Did you ever read that piece he wrote? Understand he published it in a book. Now he's paying no attention to facts or anything when he writes. But I'm never going to answer him and if I can hold to that he'll blow his top finally. Imagine the poor guy with his own personal appointment with O'Hara every day. That must be a tough one to keep each day." [As soon as he heard the erroneous initial reports of the Hemingways' death in the African plane crash, O'Hara reportedly wrote his daughter: "I really think I can get it. I want the Nobel Prize so bad I can taste it."]

"There isn't any news, Lenny. There were some funny things about the Prize business and I'll try and remember them and write them when I get home to the Finca. Better to stay down here a while, still and come in for Christmas. Juan will mail this from Havana. Merry Christmas Lenny to Sylvia and you and the boys from Mary and me, Best always, Papa."

Hemingway and my father at the Stork Club in New York, 1939.
PHOTOGRAPHER UNKNOWN

My father and Hemingway at the *Finca Vigía*, San Francisco de Paula,
Cuba, 1957. AUTHOR PHOTO

My father with Ernest and Mary Hemingway by the pool at the *Finca Vigía*. AUTHOR PHOTO

Dominic West in *Genius*. PHOTOFEST

Clive Owen on HBO's *Hemingway and Gellhorn*. PHOTOFEST

Adrian Sparks and Joely Richardson in *Papa: Ernest Hemingway in Cuba* (2015). COURTESY OF BOB YARI PRODUCTIONS

Lawrence Luckinbill as Ernest Hemingway

Corey Stoll as Ernest Hemingway in *Midnights in Paris* (2011). PHOTOFEST

VII

The year 1955 began with a letter from Mary, written from the *finca*:

> *Because Papa couldn't stand the idea of listening to an hour about himself, we put off until today playing the NBC recordings about him. As you can imagine, this kind of thing makes him itch all over his state of well-being, even when it is kind or good or flattering or true and there were parts of this which nearly brought a rash. But your part, I must tell you at once, about shooting here with the children, about the Italian taxi-driver, about "Este es el hombre" was so kind and friendly and sweet, as well as true, that I wept. From a non-weeper, it was a big, spontaneous tribute to you, Sir, and thank you very much indeed.*
>
> *Papa is working hard and sends his love and thanks you for your reiterating that he is seeing nobody. Best possible year to you all, Ever, Mary (Hemingway.)*

On May 19, 1955, Hemingway wrote again. He'd been busy writing what would be *A Moveable Feast*, a memoir about his days as a young writer and had little time for anything else. My father had written him concerning an offer to appear on *The Perry Como Show*, of all things. He wrote back:

I'm sorry that I won't be able to do it. Have decided not to go on TV until I am as fat as [Jackie] Gleason, as tactful as [This is Your Life host] Ralph Edwards or being able to show some special talent. In the meantime, am still writing books and am up to page 425 on this one.

How are you and what are your plans? Thanks for the postal card. We got it long after you were back and until I read the columns you send regularly here to the Finca. I couldn't figure out how you'd sent it. You and Sylvia certainly get around. On those high fast planes, the way my head is smashed I get deaf when they come down and it is worse every time. It is a nuisance but boats are nice anyway and we can always fly in small planes.

Wish I knew some news to send you but when you are working full-time on a book, there is no news. Just so many words a day. All good friends have been very good about letting me alone so I could write. Some other people have been very thoughtless and cash in when you are just going good and anybody coming in and interrupting when you are making up something can destroy it absolutely. If it keeps up, 'tis bad and will have to pull out for a while. If I have any luck will try to get to Africa this fall again. If I can't get there, I will find some other place. Maybe I could come up to N.Y. and we could go around on the town a little. The way we did last time and then sail on a ship when people are coming back instead of going over.

Mary is in fine health and happy and lovely but the characters that practice diurnal and nocturnal intrusions get her down.

Best to Sylvia and you and the boys, Papa

Then for some reason, he added another half to the letter:

On the health racket, I am in very good shape. Started to train and lost ten pounds and held it. Will take off ten more pounds slowly. That weight off relieves the pressure on the spine where the vertebrae are compressed and am light on my feet now and feel good." [Hemingway checked his weight every morning at the finca on an old doctor's scale and carefully noted it on the bathroom wall. The numbers still appear today—a major attraction to tourists peering in through the windows as they visit the grounds.]

Am starting to swim 440s again and coming back from down the coast steered 7 hours 50 minutes on the flying bridge without being relieved and 6 hrs. at the wheel below. I caught quite a good marlin and Mary and I caught 24 dolphins: some over twenty pounds. I wanted to test the spine out and she stood up very well. We are going out tomorrow fishing (national holiday 20th May). I don't know who the three characters are you wrote who had me ready for the glue factory. But I think you were quite safe that I could take them all right according to your conditions. Better knock on wood now and sign off. Characters can always creep up on you. Papa

In a letter dated October 22, 1955, Hemingway wrote something very touching to and about my father which I remember he proudly read to us: "Maybe you and I are the best friends we will either of us have." Then he wrote about his eldest son, John Hadley Nicanor Hemingway, who'd been nicknamed "Bumby" because of his plump teddy bear qualities. (He was named "Hadley" after his mother Hadley Richardson—Hemingway's first wife—and "Nicanor" after matador Nicanor Villalta who flourished in the 1920s when Hemingway wrote *Death in the Afternoon*.)

"This is for your personal and private information. Mr. Bumby, Miss Mary and I are in the *Floridita* in the evening. Mr. Cohn was there [Roy Cohn, the infamous lawyer for Sen. Joseph McCarthy and future Trump mentor]. I did not know him but he introduced himself as a friend of yours." [My father knew Cohn, all right, but strictly as a newsworthy person of that era. They were never friends; in fact, the night before my brothers and I had carefully prepared a surprise anniversary party for our parents, Cohn approached my father at a nightclub and said: "I heard your sons are planning a surprise anniversary party for you tomorrow night. How come I wasn't invited?" So there's the proof they were never friends!]

Hemingway continued: "Miss Mary is a little more dangerous than the average spitting cobra and likes to provoke. Mr. Bumby has a heart of gold, weighs 202 in condition and has killed more krauts, possibly than Mr. C. has intimidated witnesses and was a security officer in Berlin and has taught a long-range penetration course at Bragg where you start by jumping out of the aircraft and continue until the characters break . . . Mr. Bumby and I do not intimidate easily and both have clean hearts. So, I figured that Mr. Cohn was out of his league and slightly overmatched so I was dumb and very nice and kind. Miss Mary would fight Christ our Lord if he made one wrong move and so that is my only worry. But I do not worry."

Hemingway and Cohn apparently had made a $5 bet of some sort, but it was quickly canceled. Later he added:

You would have been proud of how we acted, I think. Maybe not proud but anyway pleased because we are more or less co-religionists. But Mr. Cohn was not coolable [sic] material. I'm pretty sure he knows it too but that is only a surmise.

*I was awfully sorry not to be able to make the fight.
Give my best to Mr. Marciano. [On September 21, 1955,
Rocky Marciano had knocked out light heavyweight champion Archie Moore in the fifth round at Yankee Stadium.]
Book at 646 [pages, not words, presumably]. It is a little
different from Mr. [Robert] Ruark [author of Something
of Value about the Mau Mau uprising in Kenya and like
Hemingway also a big-game hunter with his own ties to
Spain] less library research and 20 years' seniority. . . . But
he takes the dough and we will take the all-time prize, and
the only one I give a shit about which is honorable death
with your friends speaking well of you. Unfortunately, I
have had this small prize too so maybe we can get a new
one to hold my unflagging interest. If I were fortunate
enough to win it, we could give it to the League for the
Protection of Dissolute and outfielders. "Lenny, it was fun
to talk. Enclose five bucks to pay Mr. Roy [Cohn]. He had a
bet and we have not failed to pay one yet. The only criticism
I might make about it is that he got to the papers with it
rather fast. Best to all and Thanks, Papa."*

In 1955, Edward R. Murrow, the Babe Ruth of broad-
cast journalists, was hosting *See It Now*, which helped television news come of age. It was the forerunner of *60 Minutes*,
Nightline, *20/20*, and other in-depth network news programs
which went beyond that day's news. If you never saw *See It Now*
but did see the marvelous 2005 movie *Good Night and Good
Luck*, you know his reports on that show helped bring down the
scourge of Sen. Joseph McCarthy.

But Murrow also hosted a very different program called
Person to Person in which he brought live cameras into the homes
of well-known people. Our family had appeared on that show

on December 16, 1955. With the CBS network cameras in our apartment, my father had told Murrow he was accompanying a touring troupe of actors and singers in a production of Gershwin's *Porgy and Bess* to Russia the next day. There was only one other writer who got to make the trip: Truman Capote, who bragged that he never took notes. "I have 90 percent recall," he'd boast. What followed were columns by my father about life in the grim post-Stalinist Moscow and how Russian audiences reacted. Copies of the columns written from dreary, frigid Moscow in winter were sent to Hemingway in Cuba, which brought a thank-you letter from Mary on February 8 of the following year, 1956.

> *Dear Lenny,*
> *We can't resist writing you how interested, pleased, delighted and Papa proud (it might sound patronizing or presumptuous for me to be that) . . . about the columns, all of them without exception, about the Moscow voyage. We think they are the best series you have ever done, sound, perceptive, informative and with your sense of humor and usual lack of pretention showing through.*
>
> *For example, your line, "This is the way it's been— an individual goodwill in the collective states where our nation is marked foe." So much better than a two-column editorial. And full marks for the place and people names, which must have been a chore.*
>
> *It makes us very happy to see you growing. Best wishes to Sylvia and the boys, ever, Mary Hemingway.*

Then below Hemingway wrote: "Best luck, Lenny, been a pleasure to share your travels, Papa."

Never once did my father gloat or even reveal that the greatest novelist of the century and his wife were so impressed with his journalism. In fact, I never saw that letter of high praise until I began researching this book.

In a letter dated April 10, 1956, my father wrote Hemingway:

Dear Papa, Next Thursday and Friday, a good friend of mine will give concerts in Havana. His name is Isaac Stern. He not only is one of the world's foremost violinists, but he is also different from other musicians in that he has a great deal of warmth and goodness. From Havana he has been invited to fly to Russia for a tour.

He, of course, would be most honored if you and Mary would care to attend either of those concerts. I told him naturally, that you were busy with the new book, and that I doubted that you would find the time. But just in case you would like a little break from the daily routine, this would be a pleasant one. In any event, you would adore each other. He will be at the Presidente Hotel—of course I did not give him your number.

I read that you may be off to Peru, and another report that you would head for Africa—the first to catch a big fish; the second to find a big son. [sic] I hope both quests are successful.

Sylvia plans to leave for a quick trip to the Riviera tomorrow. I wish she could go by way of Havana, to convey to your person all our affection and good wishes.

Sincerely, Leonard

Nineteen fifty-six was a pivotal year in my life vis-à-vis our friendship with Ernest Hemingway. It would be the first trip I'd make to Spain with thirty-five more to come over the decades.

We stayed at what was then called the Castellana Hilton Hotel, where Orson Welles and his wife Paola Mori were living temporarily (everywhere Orson Welles lived was "temporary") with their infant daughter Beatrice. (There were a few glitches before the hotel officially opened. Orson, for instance, plugged his electric razor into a wall socket, and that short-circuited the hotel elevators.)

Soon after I arrived with my parents in early July, I met a beautiful twenty-one-year-old Italian actress, a Neapolitan to be precise. It was in the lobby and she happened to be staying with her sister in the room next to ours. We shared a terrace, in fact, and the next evening, she passed over a spaghetti dinner she'd cooked in her room just for me!

Her name at the time was Sofia Scicolone; she had made a few films in Italy but was then shooting her first big Hollywood movie, *The Pride and the Passion* with Frank Sinatra and Cary Grant. It was her English-language debut. I would later create the New York chapter of "The Sophia Loren Fan Club" back at my junior high school and refused to let any of my classmates join. But there was a more long-lasting effect that trip had on me. That first visit to Spain is when I saw my first bullfight. Hundreds more would ensue from a remarkable behind-the-scenes perspective, thanks to our friendship with Hemingway. More on that later.

Hemingway didn't go to Peru but passed through New York that summer. In early September, the column reported that he'd made a bet that he could stay in New York a week without anyone discovering his whereabouts—no easy task. He wanted to be free to conduct some business and meet only a few people. Somehow, Hemingway easily won his bet to be in town incognito. He stayed in New York nine days, undisturbed. Before he left, Hemingway sent Toots Shor inscribed copies of all his books. Mary added a note: "Toots, all we ask is that you please ruffle the pages—to make people think that you've read them."

That same item in the column reported the existence of a man in town who claimed Hemingway refused his challenge to a duel. "If I hit him, I'd make him famous," Hemingway explained why he declined the bizarre (and illegal) offer. "And I'm too rich to go around hitting people. But that day when I go broke, he'd better watch out."

Hemingway and my father reunited on a visit Hemingway made to New York in late August 1956. He and Mary sat with Toots Shor at his Midtown restaurant looking tanned and fit. Toots raised his glass to the Hemingways and offered his solution to all the problems of the world: "Whiskey. Booze. I think all kids should start drinking when they're six," said Shor. But Hemingway amended it by saying: "If they start with wine and water, they can never become rummies."

"His beard is now short-cropped and beginning to match the color of his hair," my father wrote. "Or maybe the other way is more accurate. His hair is beginning to match the gray of his beard. It seemed odd a few years ago when he first grew it, the dark head of hair and the long gray beard. But now it's starting to even itself out and the dividing line has faded. Mary Hemingway had just come from a session at a beauty parlor. She didn't seem to need it—trim, blond and her blue eyes twinkling. She mentioned the elephant gun again, and Papa laughed.

"'Fortunately, that gun which separated your shoulder from the recoil wasn't damaged,' he said. 'And those .577 shells still worked.'" My father continued:

The next time they'd tested the big gun was in Africa where Papa fired at an orange. It disappeared. And the third time was at dawn when the rising sun had blurred Mary's vision. She heard the sound of the Cape buffalo, an extremely dangerous animal said to have killed more hunters than any other. Hemingway wasn't holding a gun at that moment and began to shuffle weapons with the gun carrier. "We switched guns like card sharks," he said. He killed the buffalo—one shot. "The slug got through clean, maybe on to Nairobi," he said. "The buffalo went into its death dance, formed a pillar of dust, then dropped dead." [The stuffed head of that buffalo still hangs today on the wall at the Finca Vigía. Different times.] Of hunting, he said: "The English kill for sport; the Spanish kill for pride and the French kill for food."

"Never shoot unless it's at something you can take care of, or it's for the dinner table or is a dangerous beast. Otherwise, it's criminal to take a life." [The six bulls killed in bullfights are then butchered, and the meat is given to local charities.] Someone mentioned some New York gangsters and referred to them as "The Boys." Hemingway said: "Mary is such a nice girl, that whenever she hears me speak of 'The Boys' she thinks I mean my sons."

They spoke of their dog, Blackie at their home in Cuba. "Blackie's old and deaf and blind in one eye," said Hemingway. 'I wash the good eye with aureomycin four times a day. Blackie follows me around by scent. I bathe regularly but I always use the same kind of soap now and I never use any lotion so Blackie won't get confused."

Someday, he said he might accept an invitation to Russia and spend his frozen royalties in hunting such animals as the Siberian tiger [today an endangered species]. Then the talk turned to people who had recently died. Shor spoke ill of them nonetheless. "I go along with you," said Hemingway. "An S.O.B alive remains an S.O.B. dead."

Two days after that column ran, my father wrote: "For the last 48 hours, the phone at this desk has been ringing constantly, from callers who want to reach Ernest Hemingway. Old friends, self-declared friends, agents, interviewers, TV producers —all wanted to know. Hemingway is at a hideaway, relaxing. 'I just want to confuse the hell out of Celebrity Service,' he said, referring to the company which has contacts enabling subscribers to reach any well-known person."

Hemingway visited the Bronx Zoo with George Brown, at whose gym Hemingway had trained for years while in New York. "His left hook is still good, and so's his footwork," said Brown of the novelist. At the zoo that day, Hemingway identified all the birds and mammals and got close to them after the guards invited him to go inside their compounds. He talked to the hippo, imitating the guttural purring sounds they make. "I speak Hippo," he said, "but I need Miss Mary around for the grammar."

Hemingway knew Jackie Gleason. The rotund comic was then at the height of his television fame starring as bus driver Ralph Kramden in *The Honeymooners* (still seen in syndication and forever streamed on New Year's Eve on New York's WPIX-TV). He talked to "The Great One," as Gleason was called, about his long walk at the zoo. "I lost 7 pounds," said Hemingway. "For me, that's an ear lobe," replied the portly Gleason. "Just for losing that weight, I won't read any more of your books," said Gleason, feigning jealousy.

Then Gleason asked about TV reception in Cuba and Hemingway said it was poor, complaining that when he tries to watch baseball games via a station ninety miles away in Miami, he sees four pitchers and four batters each time. "I fiddle with the antenna and if I can get it down to two pitchers and two batters, I'm satisfied."

On that visit to New York, the Hemingways stayed at a friend's Midtown apartment and were the perfect guests. They left a record of every phone call they made, and left money for them. More significantly, they also left inscribed copies of all of Hemingway's books and a small painting.

A few days later, my father reported in the column that Hemingway's Nobel Prize medal would be presented to a church in Santiago, Cuba. "You really don't feel you own something," he explained "until you give it away." (Today it's back at the *finca* on his desk.)

Before he sailed for Europe on that trip, he talked of big-game hunting and then of fowl. He said that in Africa he learned how to hypnotize a chicken by placing its head under one wing, then rocking it gently.

When asked if they kept records of their conversations with their father, Hemingway's sons said they preferred telling their children about it rather than reading notes to them. "Before man learned to write," said John Hemingway, his eldest, "the stories they handed down to each other were true. The writers who wrote about it garbled it."

In late January 1957, my father was in Paris and had a reunion with the Hemingways. They'd vacationed in Spain, where he hadn't visited in several years and had vowed not to return until all his friends were out of Franco's jails. My father wrote: "It's so cold here that Ernest Hemingway wore a woolen T-shirt, sweater and cashmere robe in his suite at the Ritz Hotel." Hemingway said to my father: "'Lenny, you look like Juan Belmonte. [Belmonte was the great bullfighter of the 1920s depicted in Woody Allen's *Midnight in Paris* who revolutionized the spectacle by standing his ground and moving the bull out of his way with his cape, contrary to the ponderous style which had been in common use of getting out of the bull's way. In the movie, Allen cast a handsome Swedish actor probably because most Americans think all bullfighters are dashing like Robert Evans in *The Sun Also Rises*. But in reality Belmonte was a short, bow-legged man with one prominent feature: "It's the nose," said Hemingway. "You know what they say about noses—'Fear is in the liver, but Courage is in the nose.'"

My father said if a nose were a measure of bravery then he was "truly valorous." Then Hemingway said his nose was longer, and Mary Hemingway decided that only a formal measurement would solve the dispute. She began with Papa's, from the bridge to the tip. It measured two-and-a-half inches. Then she measured my father's which easily won at three inches. Hemingway was "crestfallen." Then, as if to find another game to win to assuage that defeat, Hemingway tossed a piece of exotic-looking soap on the hotel room floor to use as a puck for a game of foot-hockey. Then he kicked it past my father into a corner. "Not with my Italian soap!" Mary protested, ending the impromptu match.

That's when Hemingway decided to show my father around Paris, "his" Paris of his youth as a member of the famous "Lost Generation" of disillusioned poets, writers, artists, and intellectuals who came of age and flourished after World War I. The group of literary immortals included F. Scott Fitzgerald, Gertrude Stein (who coined the forlorn group's name), John Dos Passos, and T.S. Eliot.

Hemingway's tour of his old haunts began at the famous Left Bank, aka the *Rive Gauche*, where so many of that generation lived or worked. It was, in fact, where Hemingway had begun to write his classic 1926 novel about Spain called *The Sun Also Rises*. (He would use the phrase "The Lost Generation" at the end of the novel.) He told my father that after he began writing, he thought he'd saved enough money for eleven months, but the well ran dry after nine, so he worked in his spare time as a sparring partner. Once he'd tried in vain to teach Ezra Pound, the eccentric expatriate poet and critic, how to box. They'd been friends in their youth and lived near one another in Paris.

Decades later, the modernist poet and writer Archibald MacLeish wrote Hemingway. He asked Hemingway to sign a letter petitioning Attorney General Herbert Brownell to release Pound from the mental hospital called Chestnut Ward to which the fascist and anti-Semite had been confined for twelve years. Only two other names were on the petition: Robert Frost and T.S. Eliot.

"Sure, I signed the petition," Hemingway told my father. "I'm against everything Ezra Pound stands for politically, but I signed it. Pound is crazy but all poets are a bit crazy. The greatest have all been somewhat crazy. They have to be. You don't put a poet like Pound in the looney bin. For history's sake, we shouldn't keep him there. If you don't have compassion, how can you judge? I'd chip in to help support Pound after he's out," he said. "And if he starts making those same speeches again, I'd give him a spanking. But he's a poet, a bit crazy and should be let out."

As they took a taxi to the Left Bank, Hemingway said: "I used to hack around here, after the first war. That's how you get to know a city, the parts of a city. You drive a cab." As they stood at the bridge near the Place Dauphine, built by "Good King" Henry IV in 1607, Hemingway called it "a great spot to fish," pointing to the bank of the Seine. As the wind blew in whistling gusts off the river, he said, "After you get to a certain age," pulling his lightweight coat around him, "it gets into your body and finds the places where it hurts."

Hemingway maneuvered so my father would be on his right side because the hearing in his left ear was by then gone. It happened after the two plane crashes in what was then called the Belgian Congo in Africa in 1954. The doctor who treated him soon afterward had poured gin into the wound and told him: "Gin is good for you, inside and out." The wind still lashed, and my father suggested a drink. They stopped at a café and the clientele immediately recognized the distinguished customer.

As they sipped the drinks (my father was a teetotaler, so I presume it was coffee) Hemingway reminisced about his homecoming after World War I. "His mother Grace had asked him if anything had happened to him and he reassured her that his wound had been minor. His mother, thus unaware that his injuries had been serious, was under the illusion that he'd had a soft job around hospitals, rather than the dangerous job of an ambulance driver. She never could understand why he had kept his light on in his room far into the night, unable to sleep."

Hemingway then took my father to the Cluny Museum, to see the treasured medieval tapestry and the armor worn by the Crusaders. "Those men, the Crusaders," Hemingway observed, "were 5 feet 4 or 6, mostly. You can tell from the armor. They were bantam weights and feather weights for a maximum of speed. There were as few good heavyweights among them as there are today."

He then suggested a quiet bistro for lunch, and they drove near the Trocadero to Chez Ana. The first time he came there, Hemingway recalled, he'd ordered expensive dishes. Anna, the proprietor, had suggested less expensive fare, but just as filling. And if he didn't have the money, she'd trust him for it. More drinks came, and Hemingway said: "No man should drink while he has responsibility to two men, five or one hundred or twelve

85

thousand or to his wife." Then he talked about his work: "I write hardcover books for money and when I waste time, it's the kind of time-wasting a writer has to do, to get the material for his writing."

To thank Hemingway for his tour of the Paris of his youth, my father had arranged a surprise at the end of that day: a reunion across town with Ingrid Bergman. My father had been the only journalist who had defended her during the tumultuous time when she left her husband, Dr. Petter Aron Lindstrom, to run away with the Italian director Roberto Rossellini. She was vilified by the rest of the American press but my father alone wrote that that was her private life and nobody else's business. That day back in 1950, Hemingway and my father offered to act as her "seconds" should she duel with the New York press during an upcoming return to America. (She would thank my father in her 1980 autobiography, *My Story*.)

Hemingway then offered to write a story for Bergman. "Oh, please do," she replied. "It's so easy to act the roles you create. Those words you write. An actress can digest them so easily— you don't have to use any salt and pepper." Later that evening at the famed Lido nightclub, Hemingway and my father staged a "rematch" of their nose measuring contest. Only this time he used a cigarette as a measuring device. "You win," he sighed, repeating his mantra that "Fear is in the liver, but Courage is in the nose."

On August 23, 1957, the movie version of Hemingway's *The Sun Also Rises* opened. Producer Darryl F. Zanuck, whom we had visited on the set of the film shooting in Pamplona the previous July, had wanted Jennifer Jones to play Lady Brett Ashley, one of the lead roles. Hemingway, however, insisted it be his friend Ava Gardner. (Jones would've had a schedule conflict anyway, since she was filming *another* Hemingway novel, *A Farewell to Arms*.) Gregory Peck had been considered for the lead character, Jake Barnes, which eventually went to Tyrone Power.

The bullfighter in the story, called "Pedro Romero," was portrayed by a dark, handsome former women's clothing company executive named Robert Shapera. He'd been discovered by 1930s movie queen Norma Shearer sitting around the pool at the Beverly Hills Hotel. Soon, he changed his last name to "Evans" and became an actor. His first significant role was as the doomed young MGM movie mogul Irving Thalberg in 1957's *Man of a Thousand Faces*, the biography of Lon Chaney. He was a wooden, unschooled actor, but he exuded self-confidence and somehow seemed right for the role, at least to some on the set. But not all.

The cast included Errol Flynn, Mel Ferrer, and Eddie Albert, all seasoned acting pros. Some of them wanted Evans replaced, until one day the Fox studio boss Zanuck became aware of their discontent so he came to the set—then filming initial scenes in Mexico. He grabbed a bullhorn (no pun intended), turned up the volume, and barked out: "The Kid stays in the picture." That became the title for Evans's biography and 2002 documentary about his serendipitous life.

Luckily for Hollywood, in 1967, Evans showed he had other talents beyond his good, tanned looks. He took over as head of Paramount when the venerable studio was in trouble and saved it from extinction. He was the executive producer of huge box office hits in the 1970s like *Love Story*, *Marathon Man*, and *The Godfather*. Almost single-handedly, Evans transformed Paramount back to the forefront of Hollywood studios where it remains today.

Speaking of godfathers, Hemingway based the bullfighter character "Pedro Romero" on Cayetano Ordoñez, the father of Hemingway's godson Antonio Ordoñez. The real "Pedro Romero" was the first bullfighter to dismount from his horse and face a bull on foot in the ancient arena in Ronda, Spain, in 1789. The large arena is still in use today. Immortalized with Goya's paintings, it's owned by the Ordoñez grandsons, matadors Francisco and Cayetano Rivera Ordoñez. Once a year, early in September, the entire population of that mountaintop town dresses up in Goyaesque costumes and a bullfight is held with the *toreros* dressed as they did in Goya's time.

On September 23rd, 1957, Carmine Basilio upset middleweight champion Sugar Ray Robinson in a bruising split decision at Yankee Stadium. Hemingway and Joe DiMaggio were at ringside. A fan recognized "The Yankee Clipper" of course and got DiMaggio's autograph. Then he turned to the bearded Hemingway and asked: "You look familiar. I think you're somebody, right?" "Right!" replied Hemingway, "I'm Joe's doctor."

Just nine days later, on October 2, 1957, a month after *The Sun Also Rises* opened in theaters, Robert Evans attended the opening game of the World Series between the New York Yankees and Milwaukee Braves at Yankee Stadium. He spotted Hemingway seated with Toots Shor in Shor's box along the third base line, just above the visiting dugout. Just before the Yankees' star left-hander Whitey Ford went into his familiar windup, a perfectly tailored shirt cuff, in front of a perfectly cut suit jacket, and a perfectly tanned and manicured hand reached in front of Hemingway, obscuring his view. It was Evans who said: "Mr. Hemingway. I'm Robert Evans. I play the matador in *The Sun Also Rises.*"

Hemingway who had seen the rushes—the early footage—and replied: "You say you played the matador? No, you didn't."

VIII

IN MARCH 1958, MY PARENTS RETURNED TO HAVANA AND TO the *finca* for a visit. Later that day at the bar of the Havana Hilton, several American newspapermen joined them. They were questioning Hemingway about his work habits. One reporter asked: "Do you find that you write better as you get older?" Hemingway replied: "You always write as well as you can. But as you get older, you learn more, even to be afraid sometimes." Then another reporter asked if he always wrote about himself. Hemingway shrugged and replied: "Does a writer know anyone better?"

The column reported exclusively that Hemingway's vaults in New York and Havana banks, as well as the vault at the *finca*, were jammed with stories still unpublished. By this time, his next big novel *A Moveable Feast* was finished but would not be published until 1964, three years after his death. "I'm waiting," he said. "I'm waiting as I always do, to let some time pass so that I can see how much of the contemporary stuff has to be thrown away. Better that I should throw it away than posterity see it." (*A Moveable Feast* was recently republished in a digital form.)

A short letter dated April 14, 1958, arrived and Hemingway wrote: "Am working like hell. Almost certain that we can't get away in May, so you and Sylvia have the fun for us. It was

fine seeing you again as always and thanks again for the wonderful dinner. Everything quiet here."

The following April, Hemingway was back in New York,
where he lunched at Toots Shor's restaurant and signed Shor's
copy of *The Old Man and the Sea*. There was no evidence that
Shor had read the book, however. Then three young ladies at a
nearby table recognized the tanned, bearded Hemingway and
rushed out to a nearby bookstore (back when New York had a
plethora of bookstores) and brought back copies of his books to
autograph. He obliged.

The same thing had often happened to Hemingway on
other occasions. It occurred when he and a friend were driving from Venice to Monte Carlo. They stopped for lunch in
the mountain village of Cuneo, in northwest Italy located in
the foothills of the Italian Alps, south of Turin. At that time,
the population was no more than about ten thousand, so there
was only one bookstore in town. As soon as the residents recognized Hemingway, they ran to the bookstore or their homes
and brought back Italian versions of his books for him to sign.
Soon the bookstore ran out of Hemingway novels, so once the
word spread around town, late-comers began buying any book
in the store.

"I was signing all sorts of books," said Hemingway. "Books
about Galileo, to books by Clementine Paddleford," [the noted
American food writer]. "Anything."

When they reached the French border, Hemingway went
unrecognized by the guards. His somewhat disheveled garb-
scruffy pants, and ruffled shirt and an open vest-piqued their
interest, however, so they insisted on a thorough inspec-
tion. They asked him what his occupation was and Hemingway once again replied: "I write books. In stiff covers."

And speaking of autographs, Hemingway once took a drive with his close friend Gary Cooper and they stopped at a remote gas station. This was years before credit cards. Cooper paid by check, knowing that the owner of what was then called a "filling station" would never cash it so he could frame the check with Cooper's signature. "Now *you* try it," a confident Cooper said to Hemingway when they stopped at another filling station somewhere down the road.

Hemingway accepted the challenge but he lost when that owner demanded he pay in cash.

By 1958, I'd read every book on bullfighting by Barnaby Conrad. He was the author, former vice consul in Seville, amateur *torero*, owner of a popular bullfight-themed San Francisco restaurant called El Matador, and portrait artist. His books include *Gates of Fear*, *La Fiesta Brava*, *The Encyclopedia of Bullfighting*, and *How to Fight a Bull*. He also wrote *The Death of Mannolete* and recorded a dramatic version, as well as *My Life as a Matador*, a book about the famed Mexican *torero* Carlos Arruza.

I'd spent two summers living with a family with two sons my age in Madrid to improve my Spanish; you cannot fully understand the complexities of bullfighting thinking in English. Every Sunday, my friends Juan Carlos and his brother Luis José Boix and I saw bullfights in Las Ventas, Madrid's stately *Plaza de Toros* with its distinct Moorish architecture. Built in 1931, it's Spain's largest arena and the most important bullring in the world. The Boix family had a *finca* twenty-one miles north of Madrid. It was near Alcalá de Henares, the town where Miguel de Cervantes, author of *Don Quixote*, was born in 1647.

I was also learning about the various ranches, the *ganaderías* where the unique strain of fighting bulls called *Toros de Lidia* are carefully bred. Bulls from different ranches have somewhat different characteristics—similar to the way racehorses can vary from farm to farm in the United States. The matadors contract to face bulls with tendencies they know well. Some ranches, for instance, are on rough terrain and the bulls' watering place is situated some distance from their food. That way they can strengthen their legs by walking up small hills. My father had conveyed to the Hemingways my growing interest in "La Fiesta Brava" as bullfighting is called.

Thus August 9, 1958, brought a letter about this from Mary:

"Jeffrey is more informed on *toros* and *corridas* (bulls and bullfighting) than many an *aficionado* we know. We're looking forward to eating a Lyons steak at Mr. Toots' place. We both especially want to say how really excellent the columns have been. . . . Papa is still working like a fiend, so no holiday plans yet. But we hope soon."

He and Mary had been spending the winter of 1958–1959 at their home in Ketchum, Idaho, entertaining the Polish translator of his books, visiting America under a Ford Foundation fellowship. (Since they were hosting him, it's possible that Poland, despite being a Soviet satellite country, was paying him royalties. My father reported that the Russians continued to refuse to reveal how many millions of copies of Hemingway's books were sold there, since they didn't pay royalties to authors. Copies of *The Old Man and the Sea* in Germany and Poland quickly sold out.)

In early May 1959, my father ran into Kenneth Tynan, the prominent British author and sophisticated critic. He'd just returned from Cuba and said Castro had told him he'd obtained a copy of *For Whom the Bell Tolls* and took it into the hills with his men, explaining that "it was the only book in English which tells how to fight a civil war." Then Castro asked Tynan why Hemingway had never written a book about him. "He doesn't write books about politicians," Tynan told Castro. "We are not politicians," Castro replied to the journalist. "We are social reformers. Our revolution is to get the politicians out!"

Then, accompanied by his editor and close friend A. E. Hotchner, Ernest and Mary headed east toward New York but took a long detour down south all the way to the Mexican border towns. At this time, Hemingway had the last three chapters of *A Moveable Feast* to complete, so it was very unusual for him to interrupt his writing for travel. Near the Mexican border, they found a Chinese restaurant where the owner recognized Hemingway and brought out a copy of the *The Old Man and the Sea* for him to sign. It was, no doubt, the only Chinese edition of the book Hemingway would ever see and inscribe.

When they finally arrived in New York, they headed to Toots Shor's restaurant where Hemingway gave the colorful proprietor a progress report on the book. "Lemme write those last three chapters for you," Shor suggested. Hemingway nodded, saying: "That might be a good idea. I think I know how it's supposed to turn out, so maybe you can do it after all." Shor then told Hemingway he had a friend who reads a lot. Hemingway suspected the friend was single. "Any guy who reads a lot probably sleeps alone," he said. Again, different times.

Wearing his plaid cap which he often donned at that time, he and my father headed to the CBS studios to screen the videotape of his commentary about *For Whom the Bell Tolls* (not to be confused with a 1965 BBC version). Inside the studio, both Hemingway and my father took off their jackets and Hemingway noticed the magenta lining in my father's coat. He grabbed it and did a *Veronica*, one of the basic passes in bull-fighting, performed at the start of the *corrida* with the magenta and pink cape, called a *capote*. Then Hemingway spoke of Luis Miguel Dominguín, the great matador with whom he planned to travel across Spain that summer and who had had a famous affair with Ava Gardner. "It should be a great season," Hemingway predicted.

It was. Was it ever! The 1959 season—the *temporada*, in Spanish—was one of the greatest Spain had ever seen. It became the basis for *The Dangerous Summer*, initially a *Life* magazine article, but expanded to a book ("with a hard cover") detailing the historic *mano a mano* (hand to hand) appearances between Dominguín and his equally charismatic brother-in-law, Antonio Ordoñez. The book, published posthumously in 1965, recounts how all that summer, both matadors faced three bulls apiece, rather than the customary three matadors facing two bulls each. If one worked four inches from the horns, the other worked two inches away. They crisscrossed Spain, followed by hordes of international press, movie stars, seasoned aficionados, and politicians. Hemingway stood in the *callejón* giving advice to his godson Ordoñez and later proclaimed him the better *torero*. (I regret never asking Dominguín, with whom I traveled briefly in 1971, how he felt about that.)

Later that day, my father and Hemingway went to Abercrombie & Fitch to pick up two guns for his upcoming return to Africa. They were ready, protected by leather cases inscribed "E.H." and "M.H." The manager recognized my father, who'd suffered a separated shoulder the last time he was there. "How could I forget?," the manager asked, smiling.

In the restroom the attendant asked Hemingway: "Still writing books?"

"Yes," Hemingway replied again saying "with hard covers." We received a letter from him dated August 13, from Málaga, the beautiful seaside city. That was during their annual bullfight festival. It was three handwritten pages, and concerned an upcoming new edition of one of his most famous novels and a nonfiction masterpiece.

"Mary showed me yesterday the August 6th item about the *For Whom The Bell Tolls* contract ending next year and that I want it back. I can't rewrite parts of it. You are a lawyer and you know that contracts on the publication of books do not terminate that way," he wrote. "Scribner's have been my publisher since my second book and our relations are excellent and I am not rewriting any books now or in the future.

"What we are doing is writing an appendix that will run to more than forty thousand words to *Death in the Afternoon*." He added: "This will cover what happened in bullfighting from the time I left Spain to the present and will deal extensively with Luis Miguel Dominguín and Antonio Ordoñez. Various people want to publish parts of it before it comes out in the book. I may contract to write a piece for *Life* or some other outfit. That is the reason I didn't write you and give you an address since we're on the road and seeing fights in Madrid, Córdoba, Sevilla, Burgos, Aranjuez, Segovia, Alicante, Barcelona, Burgos again, Pamplona, the *férias* (festivals)of Valencia and Málaga."

That summer, historic in bullfighting history, was a series of afternoons which pitted the flashy, flamboyant style of the lanky Dominguín, with his "Suit of Lights" designed by Picasso, no less, against Ordoñez's traditional, classic dominating style. He was a classic *torero*: nothing fancy, just the ancient passes, but done with an incredible sense of mastery of the bull, combined with athleticism, his succession of passes traced back to the roots of bullfighting, the style of Pedro Romero. Hemingway used his name for the matador character in *The Sun Also Rises* but he based the character on Ordoñez's father, Cayetano. These two maestros were followed across Spain by thousands that incredible summer, chronicled by Hemingway who often stood in the *callejón* giving his godson advice. Orson Wells and other movie stars frequently attended. *Life* magazine had suggested a ten-thousand-word article and when Hemingway submitted on running much longer, his book *The Dangerous Summer* soon followed.

During one bullfight in *La Majestranza*, Seville's revered arena, Alan Lewis, the manager of the Forum restaurant in New York, sat with his wife a few seats away from Hemingway. Something happened which almost never occurs in a bullfight. One of the *toros* jumped over the *barrera*, the barrier which surrounds the arena floor. It landed in the *callejón* under the stands. On the way down, it scraped Hemingway's hand with the tip of one of its horns, causing a small gash. As his hand began to bleed, Hemingway calmly rubbed the ashes from Lewis's cigar into the wound, stopping the bleeding.

"See, Dear?" Lewis said to his mortified wife. "And you wanted me to give up smoking!"

Soon after that, Hemingway sent a letter to my father telling of a phone call he received in his home in Ketchum, Idaho, the home which he and Mary had purchased in 1959. He'd gone there to isolate himself to work undisturbed by the frequent visitors who, despite his request for solitude, would come to the *finca*. Somehow the caller had gotten ahold of Hemingway's phone number. The caller explained he too was a writer who said he'd just finished the script adaptation of his latest novel. The writer said he was worried, because the title was too long to fit on a marquee and he wondered if Hemingway could provide a shorter title.

In November, Hemingway wrote that he'd found a road sign nearby reading "Dietrich, Idaho," a tiny hamlet some 150 miles east of Boise. Hemingway gleefully posed for a photo standing in front of the sign and sent it to his good friend Marlene, addressed simply: "Dietrich, N.Y." Somehow, it arrived.

December 21, 1959, brought another chatty letter, three pages in much better handwriting than his August letter from Málaga.

"This is to wish you and Sylvia and the boys a Merry Christmas and a Happy New Year from Mary and me. We are not sending out Christmas cards this year, as Mary caught her foot and fell down and really shattered her left elbow on November 27th. She had just made a beautiful shot on an overhead high-flying pintail duck. She slipped while watching the other high-flying ducks. They operated on her at the new Sun Valley Hospital within an hour. She was lucky such a very bad break was out here instead of in a desert country.

"Anyway, she has had the finest bone surgeons there are. After Christmas they will cut the second cast off and take new pictures to see how the union is and when she can start therapy to get the arm to working. She had to have the arm straight out first and even with the second cast with the arm bent it is still in a sling. It's a long, rough deal but there could not be a better place than the *finca* and our boat, the *Pilar*, to get her sound and strong again."

A few weeks later, Hemingway wrote my father from the Sherry-Netherland hotel in New York. (Why he simply didn't call him remains a mystery.) In that letter, he sent regards to my mother "Sylvia and our six-man infield." Then he reported that Mary had broken her leg "in two places while skiing. Last year it was the right leg. This year the left. She has had the cast off a week now but it is still tender. They'd had 420 broken legs among the skiers at Cortina [Italy].

"I have the first draft of the new book all corrected and will get proofs by the first of May, probably, and Scribners plan to publish in August. Will have a chance to do some more work on the proofs. Going to be busy as a bastard here with Scribners, film decisions, etc., and am going to skip the (N.Y.) joints again. But we must get together for a tomato juice or something awful. [He would often tease my father being a teetotaler.] We had good duck and goose shooting and Venice and Paris were both as fine as ever. Am a boy with five home towns, Paris, Venice, Ketchum, Key West, and Havana. No aspersions on the other towns.

"Please give my best to Sherman [Billingsley, owner of the Stork Club]. I hate like hell not to go to the joints. But that is for afterwards, not when I'm still working. Sherman understands."

Then he reported that a favorite cat at the *finca* named "Uncle Wolfie" had died in a hurricane "and I had another cat that would train well named 'Crazy Christian', but the other cats ganged up on him and killed him. (We had better stop these sad stories.) House count: cats 58—dogs 16.

February 18, 1960, brought a letter written at the *finca* by Mary and Ernest. It came soon after they received a copy of a magazine article my mother had written called "A Mother's Prayer." Mary called it "a fine piece of work and further proof of what we already knew, that she is a first-class woman and a first-class mother." Then she wrote that "Papa has been working really hard every day since we got back from Idaho—1,536 words today, which for him is immense. He says to tell you we've had quite a few visitors lately and he will tell you about them when he sees you. He's fit and fine, swims when it's warm enough." [Her husband perused the typewritten note and in the right-hand margin wrote: "Weight 202¼ EH".]

She continued: "Our weather continues to be a moderated version of all the bad weather up north, but with records breaking here too. My thermometer slipped down to fifty-four the other night, two degrees lower than ever in fourteen years. So, little fishing, few fish." [Then Hemingway wrote here: "Still ten to fifteen degrees better than Miami. EH"]

Mary concluded with: "My good news: You have the minute distinction of being recipient of the third letter I've written with both hands since last November. 'Look, Ma—both hands.'"

Then Hemingway used the bottom half of the letter to write by hand: "Thanks for sending the clippings, Lenny. Will give you all our news when we see you. Working very hard."

The February 1960 cover of *Argosy* magazine showed a photo of Hemingway and his godson Antonio Ordoñez standing in a *callejón* beneath the title of an article called "Hemingway and the World's Phoniest Sport." Not surprisingly, Hemingway was angered when he read it, as he wrote to my father in that most recent letter: "That character who wrote in *Argosy* is a jerk who I helped to get his job. He came to Spain to do a smear job and I would not let him crash a party for the end of the bullfight season. He is pitiful and I never worried about him."

Then he put that subject aside and concluded: "Work and being straight is all that matters and I am OK no matter what you hear. Must do massage and therapy on Mary's arm now. Love to you and Sylvia, Papa. Mary's arm coming along well but weather not good yet. Will go faster when better but it's about over."

In September 1960, Hemingway was talking about bull-fighting with Carlos Arruza, Mexico's foremost matador. With his flashy style and movie-star good looks, in his day, Arruza was Mexico's answer to the sad-faced "Manolete," Spain's "Numero Uno" of the mid-1940s until Manolete was killed in the arena in Linares on August 28, 1947. (Look-alike actor Adrien Brody portrayed Manolete in an awful movie. Ironically, Arruza, despite having faced thousands of bulls, was himself killed in an auto accident while sleeping in the back seat in 1966.) Surprisingly, Hemingway wrote that he'd never seen "Manolete" perform since his heyday came during Hemingway's boycotting Franco's Spain.

"I'd say Ordoñez is the greatest," said Hemingway, "but he's my friend. About friends, you can talk very highly, but you must respect the art and the memory of others. I couldn't say Joe DiMaggio was better than Babe Ruth if I never saw Ruth play." Arruza agreed, saying: "In my garage, I have two Buicks—one from 1945, the other from 1960. Sure, they're different, but each was designed for its time."

In November 1960, Soviet First Deputy Premier Anastas Mikoyan made one of several trips to Cuba and asked local officials if he could meet Hemingway. He came to the *finca* and presented Hemingway with a set of Hemingway's works translated into Russian. Hemingway considered it a nice tribute to know that he was one of the most popular Western writers in Russia, but at the same time, he remembered no royalties ever had been paid him. So, he brought up the subject to the Soviet leader.

Mikoyan offered to arrange for those royalties to be sent, the way they finally paid W. Somerset Maugham, Sean O'Casey, and Erich Maria Remarque for their works translated into Russian. But unlike the other writers, Hemingway refused to be made another one of those exceptions. He told Mikoyan that he would accept royalties but only if all other American writers published in the USSR were paid royalties owed them as well.

Soon after that, my father reported in the column that Prince Rainier of Monaco was in town. The prince recalled to my father a dinner he'd given in the palace in Monte Carlo the previous year honoring Hemingway. The prince wanted the conversation to be lively, so he invited the witty writer Harry Kurnitz. It was a good choice. Kurnitz wrote some forty screenplays which included *One Touch of Venus*, *The Thin Man Goes Home*, and *Shadow of the Thin Man*. When it came time to toast the guest of honor, the prince drew a blank on Hemingway's name and said: "I want to toast our guest of honor . . . Harry Kurnitz." The screenwriter later proclaimed Rainier "my favorite reigning monarch." (Kurnitz later surveyed the drab-looking clientele at New York's Playboy Club, famous as a tourist trap, and said: "Christ! Somebody pulled the plug on Nebraska!")

January 15, 1961, brought a letter from Hemingway, who was at St. Mary's Hospital at the Mayo Clinic in Rochester, Minnesota.

Thank you very much, kid, for sending me [New York Times *sportswriter*] *Red Smith's and our man* [New York Post *sportswriter Jimmy*] *Cannon's columns along with yours. When the three of you are here for me to read, Rochester was a breeze. I hit here the end of November with a blood pressure of 225/125 and they have brought it down to 134/84 today. Very good people and fun to be with.*

Came into the joint under the name of my Ketchum

101

doctor, as part of the treatment was complete tranquility, and you know what luck I have with that when running under my "real" name which is "Dr. Hammerstein." Am still not giving interviews, and they are experimenting with keeping my weight down to 175—and yesterday I broke 172½—and yet may be the modern [light heavy-weight champion] Archie Moore. You never had any trouble with weight nor blood pressure, but 175 as a control factor is rough on a natural heavyweight.

Between you and me, and not to tell anybody, they found I had an incipient diabetes, controllable without insulin. Haven't told that to anybody else and know you won't. The doctor here who is handling my case is very intelligent and says there is nothing to that. Main thing is to hold the weight down for the blood pressure, keep away from the night spots and get back to my own work on which I am now nearly three months behind. Am going to keep away from all interviews, not worry about anything and give their ideas here a good try. Have a hell of a lot of work to do and want to be in shape to do it.

Hope you and Sylvia and the boys are fine and forgive no Christmas card. Will send two this year.

If you send a letter here, will probably get it, or anyway it will be forwarded to Ketchum. Best always,

Papa

Then Mary added: "Item about Rochester, Minn.—you can't find a typewriter eraser here on Sunday nights. If I could get my weight down to one ounce, I'd be in your pocket this week in Wash." [A reference to my father's attending the annual Gridiron dinner, the premier annual event for Washington journalists and politicians.]

At the bottom of the typewritten letter, Hemingway added a handwritten coda: "Sure miss you and am truly grateful for sending the columns. Better to send to Ketchum now as will be out of here probably by end of week. EH."

In May 1961, Hemingway was back at the Mayo Clinic. During his stay, on May 11, he called his good friend Gary Cooper, who was dying of prostate and colon cancer in California. Cooper ominously predicted to his old friend: "I'll bet I reach the barn before you do." He died two days later.

A. E. Hotchner was one of the last people outside the immediate Cooper family to visit the dying actor in Los Angeles. They'd hunted with Hemingway in Idaho a few years before when Cooper had discussed his plans to convert to Catholicism. During that last visit, Hotchner asked Cooper if he had any message for his old friend Hemingway. "Yes," said Cooper, clutching a crucifix. "Tell him I'm glad about this."

Three weeks before Ernest Hemingway died, Mary wrote the letter that would change my life. It was my introduction to Hemingway's godson, Antonio Ordoñez. She knew that although I was just sixteen, I was well-schooled in "The Bulls." Novelist Richard Condon had given me a detailed primer that day in 1956 in the dusty bullring of the ancient city of Toledo, some forty-five miles from Madrid. He explained everything we were watching down to the tiniest detail: the direction of the bull's charge, the different passes, the wind direction and strength, what the matador was trying to do, and a few of the subtle tricks to fool the crowd. Sure, any eleven-year-old boy from New York would find it a somewhat shocking—even mortifying—spectacle, but somehow, I was entranced in a way I will never understand.

Today I have no defense for my love of "The Bulls," as the Spaniards call it. I detest big-game hunters (including that part of Hemingway's life, in retrospect). I view today's trophy hunters as cruel yahoos, assassinating innocent animals from a long distance with no danger to themselves, wanting only to pose triumphantly over the carcass. At least Hemingway calmly faced the charge of the approaching animals he killed, standing still, until the last possible moment. He hunted elephants, Cape buffalo, and lions. He thrived on that danger, perhaps as part of his continual search for truth in the characters he created. Times change and killing big game for sport is, for me, deplorable.

But bullfighting is part of the Latin culture, dating back to ancient Crete, full of machismo and is part of Spain's psyche, however dated that may now be. Sure, it's an anachronism, and Barcelona has banned it, as much for political reasons as anything else, as that region of Spain seeks autonomy from Madrid. But I was and remain an aficionado, doubts and all. The close-up look at bullfighting I would get in ensuing summers was one few if any Americans ever experience, and it all fascinated me: the pageantry, the fear, the spectacle, and quite often the beauty in the face of death. A fighting bull or *Toro de Lidia* is arguably the most magnificent, dangerous animal on earth. It's color blind, so the expression "seeing red" to describe anger is a fallacy. Bulls aren't "angry." That's anthropomorphic nonsense. Fighting bulls have the desire to charge bred into the subspecies. On the ranch in the fields, they're actually quite docile; not "Ferdinand"-docile, but almost shy. It's the motion of the capes which, when cornered, makes it charge and try to kill with its horns. In the fields among its brothers, they're magnificent, avoiding the jeeps carrying visitors. They live years longer than beef cattle, in pastoral settings, away from any dismounted human save the *mayoral*, the ranch foreman, whom they recognize as their provider of food in the late afternoon.

Again, I have no defense, but by the same token, today's trophy hunters have none either. Nor do American bull riders in rodeos, where the belly of that type of bull is tethered with a tight rope around its waist to make it buck. Bullfighting has no place in America (although Ordoñez did cape bulls in a bloodless bullfight in the Houston Astrodome, for some reason). Although now in decline in popularity, it is nevertheless part of the soul of Spain and a few other countries, namely Mexico, Colombia, Peru, Ecuador, France, Portugal, and Venezuela.

A few days after I'd seen my first bullfight, we lunched with Orson Welles at a café in one of Madrid's innumerable town squares. Like Hemingway, Welles was a close friend of my father's apart from the journalist-interviewee relationship. He too was an expert on bullfighting (and most other subjects except for sports) and over lunch, using a stiff napkin in the sidewalk, taught me the fundamentals. Welles showed me the difference between a slow, majestic pass in which the brave matador exposes his midriff to the sharp horns passing by, and the cowardly way some *toreros* pull back at the last second, trying to look brave to the crowd; cheap tricks maybe a tenth of the audience can spot. There are other subtleties involved such as the correct area of the arena to face a particular type of bull, or dealing with changing winds which can inadvertently cause the *muleta*, the small red cape, to move suddenly, inducing an unexpected charge.

The next day, we drove to Pamplona to see movie mogul Darryl F. Zanuck, who was supervising the filming of *The Sun Also Rises*, which had begun shooting earlier in Mexico. He too schooled me on the basics.

Mary's letter to Ordoñez, in June 1961, which I've translated from Spanish reads:

Dear Antonio, A thousand thanks for your offer to come to visit Papa in the [Mayo] clinic, but we think it would be too long a trip. Now we have good news about Papa. He is improving, although a bit bored, leaving the hospital every day, swimming in a friend's pool and beginning to think of a trip to Europe in a few months. I'm going too and I hope we can spend some happy days with you all. I hope so! Papa sent me here to New York to do some business with his lawyer, banker, etc.

Here I was with a friend of ours, Leonard Lyons, a very old and dear friend of us both, who told me his third son, Jeffrey, is going once again to Spain to learn more about the country, the language, and above all The Bulls. Last summer, during his summer vacation from school, he lived with some Spanish friends near Madrid. Since he has been very young, Jeffrey has studied tauromaquia (bullfighting) and will always be so.

The father, Leonard, is a friend of ours for twenty years. He is a writer for the New York Post and is one of the most important writers in New York, a high-class person with great influence here, with great friendship for us, who has done many kind things for us. In regard to that, he's also a friend to everyone—Winston Churchill and President Kennedy, Sophia Loren, Marilyn Monroe and Brigitte Bardot. His wife is also a very good person and a great friend of ours.

Young Jeffrey speaks and writes English and Spanish and can translate both languages and write on his typewriter in both languages. He's seventeen [I was fifteen], is a strong boy who weighs 70.7 kilos and eager to work hard. [How did Mary know my weight?!]

Papa thought you would like to bring him along in your cuadrilla *[a matador's group of assistants] for this summer. It is the hope of his life that he could go with you to Pamplona and be there for the Festival of San Fermin.*

Papa told me that whatever favor you can do for this boy, he will be very happy and grateful. Me too.

Jeffrey will arrive in Madrid at the end of this month and I will give him another letter presenting him personally to you.

A dozen kisses to you and Carmen and great luck,
Mary

(I never heard my father so much as mention Brigitte Bardot, much less anything about a friendship. I wish he had!)

I later learned that Hemingway imagined that I would spend just a few weeks touring with Ordoñez—like a roadie for the Rolling Stones, or a batboy for my beloved Boston Red Sox on an extended road trip. That first trip to Spain lasted the entire summer of 1961, to be followed by six others with Ordoñez over the next decade. We crisscrossed the Iberian Peninsula in his troupe of three cars, about two thousand miles a week. In the process, I also acquired a "brother-from-another-mother," one of the most amazing men I ever knew. Although the only words in English he ever bothered to learn were "Ok, Mac," Antonio could find a Spanish-speaking waiter at, say, a diner in remote Idaho and had explored the far reaches of Brooklyn neighborhoods most Manhattanites like me have never seen.

Antonio Ordoñez was by far the bravest man I ever knew as well. I'd read all about him long before we met; he looked more like an athlete than a bullfighter: a well-conditioned halfback who had endless charisma. Seat him in a restaurant in Kathmandu, Nepal, for example, and people would somehow know there's someone special in the room.

Armed with a copy of Mary Hemingway's letter, I arrived at his home in late June, fresh off the Iberia flight from Idlewild (now JFK) to Madrid, not quite knowing what to expect. He and his wife Carmen (sister of his rival Luis Miguel Dominguín) had two small daughters named Carmen and Belén. I would come to know them well in ensuing years. Both daughters would die in early middle age. In 1984, Carmen's former husband, Francisco Rivera, known by his nickname, "Paquirri," a popular and beloved matador, would be killed in the arena, a very rare occurrence since the discovery of penicillin in 1928. The bull was named "Avispado," which means clever in English. From what I could discern from a video, the *toro* had given him a warning of sorts, jerking its horns up after a pass that he'd done dozens of times before without any consequences. But something freakish happened; perhaps he'd lost concentration for an instant. Serious gorings are extremely rare and always seem to happen in smaller arenas where there are no horn wound specialists. That's how "Manolete" had been killed in 1947. "Paquirri," a charming young man, was honored with one of Spain's largest funerals.

After that happened, Carmen, Antonio's older daughter, vowed that their two sons, Francisco and Cayetano, would never be allowed to become matadors, the family legacy notwithstanding. To that end, she asked us to find a summer camp for them, to get them away from Spanish traditions. They thus spent the summers of 1987–1989 at a camp we found in Maine and weeks with us before and afterward out on Long Island. But when I saw Francisco practicing passes with my souvenir cape on our front lawn on Long Island one night, I knew his mother's plan would fail. It was in their DNA. Both brothers became famous matadors in the family tradition and in fact were the subject of two pieces on *60 Minutes*, the second a full hour called "Blood Brothers" narrated by the late correspondent Bob Simon.

An hour or two after my arrival at the Ordoñez home, we left Madrid for the long drive to the dusty city of Alicante for his bullfight the next afternoon. It was a 258-mile drive, with me fresh off a transatlantic flight. It was on-the-job training in living out of a small suitcase, since every day would involve a long drive after the bullfight. Along the way, I remember feeling a touch of home listening to Antonio's Nat "King" Cole records on a built-in turntable just under the dashboard of his customized Citroen, a bulky-looking but comfortable French car. For Antonio, the turntable was a proud possession, since it was installed with springs above and below it, and thus immune to the bouncing caused by the rough roads which crisscrossed Spain in its pre-highway days.

We would drive all night from one end of the Iberian Peninsula to another, following the various cities' annual bullfight festivals. During the drives, there would inevitably be a stop at an isolated bar/restaurant up in the hills which always seemed to have on display a life-sized portrait of Antonio, who I'm certain was comped for the meals. I would pepper him with questions about how his bulls turned out and he never seemed to tire of that, lacing his replies with humorous asides.

Every midnight while driving along the endless, dimly lit roads which crosscross the Iberian Peninsula, we'd tune into the national radio network out of Madrid to listen to the results of other bullfights. The report gave descriptions of how well or poorly other big-name matadors fared, gaged by the audience reaction and how big the crowds were and from which ranches the bulls came. Although bullfighting is often mistakenly called a sport, it isn't, but the nightly bullfight news was akin to today's ESPN *SportsCenter*.

Antonio loved "Ernesto," and spoke with me often about their friendship. Though short on formal education, Antonio was a very astute, always-curious wise man, who loved teasing me about my reluctance to eat foods unknown to me since I'd had some digestive issues in previous summers in Spain. All that summer, I stuck to a *"filete y* Coca-Cola," or steak and Coke diet, which made for endless ribbing which in retrospect, I deserved.

On days when he was fighting (for want of a better word in English) he would eat lightly in case he was gored and needed surgery. That's a common practice of all *toreros*. I noticed his body was covered with scars: forty or so, he told me. Each one was from a different goring in a different arena. In the late mornings of every bullfight, the matadors try to relax in their hotel rooms, greeting friends or consulting with aides on the design of new suits. A small portable chapel is on the desk, and I would always leave early to give well-wishers some space. It was off to the arena to see the *sorteo*, the ritual sorting of that afternoon's six bulls into individual pens. First the bulls—six to a lot—are taken out of the heavy boxes which brought them from distant corners of Spain but usually from the South, in *Andalucía*. Sometimes they've been there in the back corrals at the arena for several days, but always placed with their brothers to keep them calm.

Reporters and friends come by to inspect them and make notes about things like size, muscle configuration and the all-important shape of the horns. Then in the early afternoon, Antonio would take a short nap before praying to the Virgin of the Macarena. She's the bullfighters' patron saint, and they pray at the impromptu shrine with religious icons. After that, his *mozo de espada*, his sword handler/valet Curro Puya, would come for the ritual dressing of the matador in the Suit of Lights, or the *Traje de Luces*. The matadors wear tight Bolero-style jackets with high sleeves and the gold sequins are made of gold. The assistants, or *bandilleros*, wear such suits as well, but their decorations are made of silver. That takes almost half an hour and is laced with tradition.

Then it was off to the arena. I'd often ride with him and his assistants with the van surrounded by fans all along the way—think of the Beatles besieged by screaming fans in *A Hard Day's Night*—the trappings of a national hero. Today his grandsons, Francisco and Cayetano, get the same adulation.

I'd find my seat, usually in the *callejón* passageway, and join him back at the hotel afterward. I'd often sneak a look at him in the passageway on the other side of the arena to try and gage his mood. Would he recognize a good, brave bull and perform as only he could? Or would he draw a slow, cowardly bull who had to be drawn to the cape and he'd thus deliver a ponderous performance? You could never tell.

I tried to blend in with the breeders, reporters, and others in that world—some of whom I knew—though a Boston Red Sox cap may have given me away as an American. Later, assuming he hadn't been caught by the horns, if he'd drawn willing, brave bulls and had done well, he'd spend an hour or so lounging in his hotel room on the phone and accepting congratulations from friends. One call was always from his wife Carmen (appropriately named for a matador's wife!), who almost never saw him perform due to a long-standing superstition.

If he'd had a bad afternoon, we'd always leave town quickly, headed to the next city on the schedule.

There were two other cars in his mini caravan. I often rode in the middle one, a gray Mercedes, along with his brother Alfonso, and we would inevitably spend the long overnight drives arguing politics of the day. By the summer of 1970, however, my last full summer touring with him, we would engage in fierce debates. I attacked the then-president so often and so passionately, not realizing I was sometimes being egged on, the bullfighters began kiddingly calling me "Nixon."

The most fun was when I was assigned to travel in the third car, a clunky old black DeSoto limousine which had a top speed of about fifty miles per hour. Good thing, because in those days, Spain's highways weren't yet modernized and many roads were narrow, bumpy, and twisting. Decades before satellite radio, that limousine did at least have a shortwave radio. Late at night when the reception was best, I would tune into Armed Forces Radio to get baseball scores and even an occasional game, live from back home! I could hear, for instance, the familiar voice of Hall of Fame Yankee shortstop-turned-announcer Phil Rizzuto calling a game.

On July 19, 1964, during my next summer with Ordoñez, on another endless drive to the next city, while only the driver and I were awake, I tuned into a game and listened to a young Cuban pitcher named Luis Tiant throw a shutout for Cleveland against the Yankees. My explanation of an earned run average or on-base percentage and other complex nuances of baseball, may have left something to be desired, but the other bullfighters, who'd awakened, got the general idea. Years later, at Red Sox spring training, I told Tiant I'd heard his debut in the middle of the night from somewhere in Spain! He then recited all the details of that game.

One time in 2010, our son Ben and I went to the *sorteo* with the *cuadrilla* of Antonio's older grandson, Francisco Rivera. As we looked over the bulls in one large pen, one of Francisco's men asked *me* what I'd thought of them! At the expense of sounding self-serving, that was quite an honor. Apparently, Francisco had told them of my summers with Antonio and that he thought my opinion would be helpful. I remember thinking I'd better be careful when I spoke, since their lives could depend on it to an extent, so I told them simply they were "impressive." and left it at that.

Sitting among the *ganaderos*—the breeders—close to the arena I'd be on edge whenever Antonio and later Francisco and brother Cayetano were close to the horns. One wrong step, one slip on the sand, one sudden gust of wind blowing the red *muleta* unexpectedly and they could find several inches of sharp horn in their body. It is a terrible yet exhilarating way to live. But Antonio personified some of Hemingway's attributes: pursuing the truth, courageously facing death, and living life to the fullest.

That winter of 1961 like many top matadors, he'd fought in Mexico and South America and passed through New York on his way home. My father took him around town one night, introducing Ordoñez to all the newsworthy people who were out and about. It was the year of the Twist craze, so they stopped at the Peppermint Lounge on West 46th Street, the epicenter of that dance fad. My father, the winner of the P.S. 160 Spanish Prize pin of 1919 (which he wore to a white tie dinner at the White House where the invitation had read "Decorations will be worn") spoke Spanish with Ordoñez. *"Dos semanas como un camarero seria todo lo que necesito para aprender Ingles,"* said Ordoñez, expressing his envy for the waiters who had quickly learned English in two weeks.

At another nightspot, my father introduced him to Marlon Brando, who Ordoñez called "the Dominguín of actors." Brando knew who Antonio was, but didn't get the comparison. "So, if he's like Dominguín, who are you?" my father asked Antonio. Ordoñez smiled and replied, "Paul Newman!"

As they walked the darkened streets of Manhattan, their talk turned to Hemingway and Ordoñez recalled how while he was appearing in the city of Murcia, someone had broken into his hotel room and stolen the gold money clasp he'd been given by Hemingway. So he called a press conference and mentioned the loss and desire to recover only the clasp with its etched stamp of the Virgin de la Macarena.

Eight days later, the money clasp arrived in the mail in an envelope addressed only to "Antonio, Madrid." When he told that story to his good friend Anthony Quinn, they began comparing their reputations. They walked into a bistro where everyone recognized the Oscar winner Quinn—then at the height of his fame as a film star—and began applauding. "Yes, I noticed that," Ordoñez teased Quinn, "but they all know I don't like people to applaud me outside the bullring."

Their last stop was P.J. Clark's, the famous bar where the watershed 1945 movie *The Lost Weekend* was filmed. Ordoñez, who'd temporarily retired to raise bulls and grow olives, ordered a vodka martini. *"Y no se olvide la aceituna, por favor,"* he told the waiter. "And don't forget the olive, please."

One memorable day at his ranch in Carmona, near Seville, we walked into a large corral with about twenty fully grown

114

five-year-old bulls, each close to one thousand pounds. One or two looked up at us momentarily, and probably realizing we posed no threat, continued grazing contentedly. "Just walk slowly and keep your voice down," he cautioned. It was one of the scariest yet thrilling moments of my life!

Later he told me he remembers the faces of every one of the more than three thousand bulls he faced in his long career. "*Es imposible*," I replied. Then he said: "If your life depended on twenty minutes of intense concentration, you'd remember every second."

My father arranged a private tour of the United Nations for Ordoñez which included a meeting with then-Secretary General U Thant. Ordoñez told the diplomat: "I owe this moment to the bulls. If I hadn't been a *torero*, I'd have been a bootblack back in my hometown of Ronda shining shoes for a living."

Our friendship would last for thirty-seven years with his occasional visits to New York, and visits by my wife Judy and me to his ranch in Carmona near Seville in later years. I have fond memories of a friendship I forged between Antonio and Frank Gifford, perhaps the New York Football Giants' greatest all-around player. I was the translator as they swapped war stories one night at P.J. Clark's, two immortals of their fields.

Six months before Antonio died of lung cancer in December 1998, he came to New York to be treated at the famous Sloan-Kettering cancer center, and I took that opportunity to fulfill a longtime dream: I took him and his second wife Pilar Lezcano to a baseball game. At that time, the New York Mets had a slick-fielding but light-hitting Cuban shortstop named Rey Ordoñez, and before the game, I introduced them, and to manager Bobby Valentine, and former Met-turned-announcer Keith Hernandez, whose ancestry is from Spain. He even got to meet former Yankee shortstop and General Manager Gene Michael; worlds colliding. Mets third base coach "Cookie" Rojas, another Cuban, had vacationed postseason in Spain and knew who Antonio was and how great his stature was. He told his young shortstop: "If you play baseball the way he fought bulls, you'll be in the Hall of Fame."

IX

Three months after Hemingway died, Mary was back in Ketchum and wrote a long, heartfelt letter to my father. She had just returned from Cuba after getting special permission from President Kennedy to travel there despite the recently instituted embargo.

I'm sorry your son George and his pretty bride Robin got cheated out of their wedding present, but I will, sooner or later, send them a substitute which I hope will be acceptable.

Valerie Danby-Smith [Hemingway's Irish-born assistant who would marry his youngest son Gregory] and I worked 12 to 14 hours nearly every day for five weeks in Cuba sorting out Papa's papers—you know he never threw away even magazine wrappers. Then we shipped them to Tampa, then made an inventory of everything in the house except the books (more than 5,000 with a very high percentage, more than half, I estimate, of the sort that would be useful for various branches for research—biography, history, botany, oceanography, anthropology, astronomy, entomology, ecology, art, geography—about half in English, the other half in Spanish, French and Italian).

The original Cuban idea was to make our home a museum, but I urged them to make it a study center so that the books would be useful instead of merely ornamental and the Prime Minister agreed. Incidentally, it was only with his personal help that I was able to send north all but one of our pictures.

The Finca as you saw it last and remember it remains as always. Of the 86 heads in the house, I brought away only 3—Papa's favorite impala. Three fine ones remain there: my Lesser Kudu [his Greater Kudu remains in the dining room where it always hung] and a little Tommy [a Thompson gazelle] I had in my bedroom to remember the day we tracked him for about ten miles. I did a history of each remaining head and how it was acquired, also in any pamphlet they get about the place, telling how Papa and I lived there.

If this gets out, I suppose some people will renew their judgements that I am pro-Communist and off my rocker and irresponsible, etc. Some papers did when I went down there. That won't bother me too much, since our government and the British MI5 know all about me, i.e. I've never been a member of any political party or other organization including the Newspaper Guild.

What does *bother me are the people deploring the fact that I am destroying Papa's work and imploring me not to burn any of the documents. That sort of impassioned plea I find ignorant, preposterous and ridiculous, particularly the idea that I could be so presumptuous as to "alter" anything of Papa's. From Cuba I wrote to Scribners asking them to allay their fears.*

After Hemingway died, my father wrote several columns and magazine articles about their friendship. One recalled an incident one night in the Stork Club, where a lawyer sat down—uninvited. He kept touching Hemingway's face while he kept talking. "Stop that!" said Hemingway. But the lawyer, who had downed a few, did it again. Hemingway half-rose from his seat and grazed the man's jaw with a short right, probably suspecting the tipsy lawyer was at a disadvantage.

The lawyer fell off the chair, was helped to his feet, and both men shook hands. Then the lawyer fell down again. He arose, muttered something about having $3,000 on his person and told Hemingway to feel his muscle. "You're not so tough," he said. "Let's fight." Hemingway told him: "For $3,000, I'd fight anybody. I'd fight you for $50. But you're a good guy, and good guys shouldn't fight. But if you want to fight, let's go into the men's room or call me at my hotel tomorrow." Then he took off his glasses, gave them to my father for safekeeping, and stood up. The lawyer, thinking better about things, realized Hemingway would be a formidable opponent, and staggered off.

Another story concerned a flight Hemingway took home from China before the Pearl Harbor attacks. His traveling companion was a man named Bernt Belchen, a noted Norwegian-born aviator and winner of the Distinguished Flying Cross. He'd trained as a boxer hoping to make the 1920 Norwegian Olympic team. The long flight across the Pacific had a refueling stop at Wake Island, which would soon come under heavy air attack by the Japanese. Belchen also told Hemingway he'd been an Olympic wrestler. In their quarters, the Pan-Am frame house, built on stilts, these two barrel-chested men couldn't resist the temptation to square off. They wrestled all over the house, shattering the interior. Only the announcement that their plane was refueled and ready for departure ended the match in a draw.

Hemingway told my father that while he and Martha Gellhorn were living in Key West, he began each day doing one hundred sit-ups with his knees straight out. "I like Key West," he said. "It's the kind of town a fighter says he's from."

Hemingway dealt with fame in many ways. Although being world-famous surely helped sales of his books, he nevertheless shunned TV appearances, but would sign books when requested by fans. But his patience had limits. As is the case with athletes, he disliked being bothered while he was eating in restaurants. So did Mary. One night late in 1952, she dined with A. E. Hotchner, an author and Hemingway's editor and confidant. (He would live to be 100¾ before his death on February 15, 2020.) A stranger came along, introduced himself, and asked: "Mind if I sit down?" Then, without waiting for an answer, the intruder grabbed a chair and sat down. Mary later recalled that her husband had many encounters with such people whom he derisively called "joiners."

In Havana one night, another joiner boldly sat down at their table, uninvited of course. He then started saying all the wrong things. Mary became incensed at such rudeness during their meal. She remembered the punch-throwing lessons her husband had taught her. "So, I first removed my shoes," she recalled, "because you can't punch hard in high heels. And I hit him! He left."

Hotchner then recalled yet another joiner who was effusive in his praise of Hemingway's books. My father was sitting with them (invited, of course!). "My wife and I are great admirers of yours," said the joiner. "She's sitting right over there. We've read everything you ever wrote; books, short stories, you name it. Everything. Your book, *All Quiet on the Western Front*—great, great book; greatest war novel ever written."

That *was* indeed a great novel—written by Erich Maria Remarque!

"Yes, it is a great novel," replied Hemingway, patiently, no doubt either suppressing a laugh or controlling his urge to slug the man. But the joiner wasn't finished.

"And that other great book of yours, Mr. Hemingway—my favorite," he continued. "Oh, you know which one; I can't think of the title."

"*Of Mice and Men?*" Hemingway suggested. "Yes, that's the one," replied the joiner, surely relieved that his temporary amnesia had been cured, even though John Steinbeck had written that one.

"And then there was *The Bridge of San Luis Rey*, Mr. Hemingway," he continued. "A classic." Of course, that was the outstanding novel by Thornton Wilder. Finally, after the buffoon praised Hemingway for his "masterpiece: *The Grapes of Wrath*," saying it captured the tragedy of the Great Depression, he said: "Why don't you come over to my table and meet the wife. It would thrill her. Really would." Amazingly, Hemingway—by this time seething—accompanied the joiner to the other table. When he returned, Hotchner asked: "Why the hell didn't you tell him off—that you didn't write any of those books?"

"That would've been easy," replied Hemingway. "No, my way is better. He'll get what he deserves tomorrow when he no doubt starts repeating this incident verbatim to his friends. They're bound to correct him and they won't believe him at all."

Sometime in 1960, "The Lyons Den" carried an amazing story about how Jack Hemingway—who parachuted into occupied France with his fishing rod, reel, and gear, true to family form—survived being a POW during the war. Lt. Jack Hemingway and two French resistance fighters reached what they thought was a rendezvous point only to be hit by enemy fire. One of the Frenchmen was killed. Hemingway and the other man were wounded and captured. The Germans were commanded by an Austrian officer who grabbed Hemingway's dog tags and asked him: "Were you ever in Schurnz?" the officer's hometown. "Yes," replied Hemingway, surprised by the question. Many years before, Ernest Hemingway had worked there as a ski instructor and his son was living there with his father. The officer then ordered the wounded younger Hemingway sent directly to a hospital, avoiding intense interrogation, even torture, which might've brought out that he was working for the OSS, the precursor of today's CIA.

Ernest Hemingway lives on, of course, through his classic works (the ones he really did write!). But he has also come alive onstage and in movies. He has an uncredited cameo with Mary in the screen version of *The Old Man and the Sea* as one of the patrons at an outdoor bar on the beach early on. There's also a select group of actors who have portrayed him in one-man shows and in at least one feature movie about his time in Cuba.

Hemingway lived into the formative years of television but made only a few appearances, alas. Today, he can be seen in a short, somewhat stilted video on YouTube. It was filmed in 1954, after he won the Nobel Prize in Literature. The interviewer, an NBC reporter, looked nervous and unprepared, perhaps awestruck. Hemingway's responses are almost robot-like. But it does give a hint at his Midwestern twang and slightly high-pitched voice.

In addition to that 1954 interview clip, YouTube has some clips of Hemingway and the movie he produced in 1937 about the Spanish Civil War called *The Spanish Earth*. He also served as narrator along with Orson Welles and director Jean Renoir.

X

Several noted actors have portrayed Hemingway, and the portrayals I've seen managed to capture his presence, in one way or another, a testament to the Hemingwayesque dialogue and their skills.

British-born actor Clive Owen played Hemingway during the Spanish Civil war on HBO's *Hemingway and Gellhorn*, with Nicole Kidman costarring as Martha. Owen captured Hemingway at the halfway point in his life. Phillip Kaufman whose resumé includes *The Right Stuff* directed.

"It was a difficult time in his life," Owen recalled to me. "Both he and his wife were drinking and fighting a lot and were competitors reporting for different outlets, which only made things more intense."

Hemingway and Gellhorn aired in 2012 and depicted the intense rivalry between the two, since both Hemingway and his then-wife, globe-trotting journalist were covering the bloody conflict in Spain for competing magazines. At the time of production, Owen hadn't read much Hemingway, but quickly began preparations.

"I was shocked that Phil asked me to play Hemingway," Owen told me. "He must've seen something in me which convinced him I was right for the part. You can't play somebody like Hemingway and treat it like you do every other film. I just immersed myself for eight months with everything

Hemingway—everything he wrote, everything that was written about him. I visited Madrid, Paris, and Cuba. In Paris at the Hemingway bar, I told them who I was about to portray and they let me see a book of family photos which helped me enormously. I saw all the places he went and where he'd lived.

"I also went to the home in Cuba which was then undergoing renovation and restoration. I was amazed. All those books still on the shelves and even the clothes in the closets! It's as if he was still there." Like the actors before and after him, Owen, who does a convincing American accent, left it at that, deciding not to imitate Hemingway's surprisingly high-pitched almost nasal Midwestern tone.

As for rehearsing before shooting, Owen said: "I'm not one for over-rehearsing. That's OK for theater, where every night has to look fresh, but in film, you have to be able to do it once, if possible.

"I came away from that role and began reading all his works and was amazed at the incredible economy of his words. That was one of the keys to his greatness as a writer."

Although filmed in and around San Francisco, the landscape suggested Spain during that brutal war.

Len Cariou, the powerful Canadian-born actor, is best known as Broadway's original "Sweeney Todd" and more recently as the cantankerous but wise great-grandfather and former New York City police commissioner Henry Reagan on CBS's long-running show *Blue Bloods*. He portrayed Hemingway in a one-man show called *Papa* which had a well-received run off-Broadway in April 1996. The set was a replica of the *finca* which I remembered as being accurate.

I took our son Ben, then fourteen, to see the play called "Papa," and afterward, reunited backstage with Cariou, an old friend and rival from the Broadway Show League softball games in Central Park. Written by John DeGroot, *Papa* began as a staged reading in Key West, one of Hemingway's "home-towns" and then in Fort Lauderdale. The late George Peppard also toured with the play in 1988. The play was set at the *finca* on an evening in August 1959, soon after he'd returned from Spain covering the *mano a mano* bullfights between Ordoñez and Dominguín—"The Dangerous Summer."

Cariou remembered our visit backstage and how I'd told Ben that since our visit was twenty-nine years before he was born, this was the next best thing. And it was, because Ben really seemed to get a sense of Hemingway and the *finca*.

"I'd always been a fan of Hemingway's writing," Cariou told me. "So, there wasn't much hesitation about doing the play. I'd seen *The Sun Also Rises* and read the book, and I was never afraid I couldn't get him; get inside him. I didn't want to re-create his high-pitched voice, because it didn't fit the image, so I just used my own way of speaking." And he succeeded in re-creating Hemingway at a pivotal time in his life, when he the author was said to have self-doubts, was depressed, and feared writer's block. His health was about to decline as well.

Another actor who took on the role was Adrian Sparks, a long-time stage actor with lots of TV and occasional screen credits as well. His resumé includes appearances on *The West Wing*, *Curb Your Enthusiasm*, *The Young and the Restless*, and *NCIS*. Sparks came to the role in a most unusual way.

125

"I was working at the Globe Theater in San Diego," he told me, "and backstage I got a call from someone about doing this play on Hemingway. I didn't think the call was for real, since producers routinely call actors' agents first to see if there's any interest. In fact, I thought it was a prank by some of the stage-hands who thought I looked so much like him. So, I remember saying 'Thanks for the interest. Talk to my agent,' then hung up and thought nothing of it.

"Then a year later I got another call from the same guy and began to realize this was for real! '"Why *not* jump at it?' I remember thinking. After all, reading Hemingway's books got me through puberty!

"This time the play was directed by Martha Damson and her process was different from other directors. It gave me a new perspective. I was able to explore the emotions I thought were inside him. His language and sudden mood shifts are so muscular; it's such an overpowering presence. That's why I was going after his vulnerabilities and his fears late in his life. He'd survived death in war, exposed himself to danger in hunting, in looking the bull in the eye. It became a powerful journey."

Sparks would perform this version of *Papa* everywhere, including of all places Turkey where it ran, Turkish subtitles and all, for six months!

Then along came director Bob Yari with a completely different script for a movie called *Papa, Hemingway in Cuba* which opened in the spring of 2015. To everyone's amazement, Yari obtained permission to film not just in Havana, but inside the *Finca Vigía*! As luck would have it, the *finca* had recently been restored by a government project headed by the renowned TV home renovator, Bob Vila, the Miami-born

Cuban-American who hosted popular home renovation shows *This Old House*, *Home Again with Bob Vila*, and *Restore America*. Director Yari had prepared duplicate sets of everything, just in case there was a hitch in getting permission, Sparks said. Then came the good news from the Cuban government. "Before I knew it," Sparks recalled, "we were filming in Hemingway's dining room, and I was seated next to his granddaughter Mariel, who had a cameo as a dinner guest! They even let me use his typewriter! Half the crew was Cuban, so we really had a feel for things. At first, they were suspicious of this guy who looked so much like Hemingway. Ada Rosa Rosales, the director of the museum at that time, was skeptical, too. She kept her arms crossed and I avoided her at first, keeping an eye on everything. But after a week, she came around. Still, I noticed there was always an attendant there, closely watching what we were doing.

"My only thought was 'What am I doing here, clacking away on this great man's typewriter; the very one he used writing *The Old Man and the Sea*?!'" (Hemingway had told my father he was a bit superstitious about his battered typewriter, for it had brought him such success.)

One scene in the movie was a shoot-out between the corrupt Cuban dictator Fulgencio Batista's soldiers and Castro insurgents. It happened in front of the presidential palace. It still stands today as a tourist attraction, along with the bullet holes visible in the walls. You can visit the building and see Batista's office, untouched since the dictator fled Cuba on December 31, 1958, the day before Castro and his men rolled in.

Giovanni Ribisi costarred in the movie portraying the Miami-based newspaper reporter in the story written by Denne Bart Petitclerc. In real life, he did befriend Hemingway just as the Cuban revolution was unfolding. In the movie, his character, called "Ed Myers" (for some reason), and Sparks were seen caught in the crossfire of that shootout outside the presidential palace. Hemingway and the reporter were pinned down just out of range of the barrage between soldiers and Castro insurgents.

"I had a day off from filming," Sparks recalled, "and a seventy-year-old woman approached me. She told me she'd been there that day and our re-creation looked authentic and that watching the scene being filmed brought it all back for her."Another thing that attracted him to the project was that "Hemingway was one of the first guys to write about a man in love having an emotional connection to being in love." The movie also captured his dramatic emotional swings, in the scene re-creating a large luncheon at the *finca*. "*That* was sort of surreal," he recalled.

Sparks also faced the dilemma of trying to capture Hemingway's voice. "Yes, the voice was a point of discussion," said Sparks. "With both my stage and screen directors. In both cases, we felt it would create an unnecessary distraction if I tried to imitate his somewhat high-pitched nasal Midwestern speech, without some sort of textual reference. We took some solace in the fact that in many ways, my voice is similar to his."

Sparks, though born in England, grew up in Waukegan, Illinois, not far from Oak Park where Hemingway was born in 1899. (Waukegan is also the hometown of comedian/actor Benjamin Kobelski, better known as Jack Benny.) "In fact," Sparks said, "our Waukegan high school teams played Oak Park in several sports. So, there is definitely that Midwestern nasal high-in-the-throat quality in both of our voices. Nevertheless, one critic who didn't get the film at all, denigrated my performance, saying my voice wasn't *deep* enough! So, what are you going to do?

"A significant part of my experience was to realize what an extraordinary impact he had on everyone he ever met. Everyone in Havana, it seems, has a Hemingway story, and most of them never knew him or were born after he died. And I think I got to hear all their stories. People would push past my costar Giovanni Ribisi to get to me because I look so much like him.

"One afternoon, we were filming in Cojimar, the fishing village part of the district of Havana, which inspired *The Old Man and the Sea*, I was standing out on the dock where Hemingway had stood and we heard a scream. It was an old lady on crutches holding out her arms to me. I went to see her and through a translator, learned that when she'd been a little girl, she'd stood outside the gate of the *finca* and saw Hemingway. All she said was: 'Usted!' 'You!'"

Director Yari agreed that imitating Hemingway's pitch would have been a needless distraction. As for re-creating his voice, he explained that "sometimes you have to take a bit of poetic license and veer slightly away from reality. Having seen Adrian as Hemingway onstage, I was struck by the power of the performance and my thought was: 'Don't mess with this.' Simple as that."

As for the reaction to the film, he said he'd "received a high number of very long letters detailing how important Hemingway was to them."

Sparks's costar in the movie was Joely Richardson, who portrayed Mary Walsh Hemingway. The actress, whose resumé includes the 2011 English-language version of *The Girl with the Dragon Tattoo*, *101 Dalmatians*, and *Drowning by Numbers*, is a member of the famed Redgrave family of actors. She felt that initially the script was "wordy" and "it painted Mary in a very bad light. I had a feeling she was complicated but the thought of going to Cuba to the real home and attempting to re-create Hemingway and his wife was too great an opportunity to turn down," she told me. "Little did I realize it would be exactly as it was in the home when they lived there. Everything was still there, all the knickknacks." She also got to swim nude in the Hemingway pool, just as Ava Gardner had famously done.

Her problems with her character persisted, however. "We tried to rewrite as we went along," she recalled. "I begged to give Mary a few more shades. But it was one of the best experiences I had with the actors, with Cuba, the director and all. Nevertheless, there was only so much we could do and still I feel she was painted a bit too harshly. I'm guessing it was the mix between them that was tricky."

But then she added: "This is all in retrospect. It's a terrible thing to pass judgment on someone you didn't know. It seems to me that Mary had problems. Everyone drank way too much. I'm about a foot taller than she but seeing a Hemingway at the lunch table (Mariel) was special. But then the boat wasn't ready so we used a replica of the *Pilar*. I've reread *The Old Man and the Sea* and feel how lucky we were to embrace these people's lives. The experience was an enormous gift."

Veteran Stacy Keach took on the role in a stage production. Keach, perhaps best known as TV's Mike Hammer and for a slew of movie roles, is currently performing the play and has a recurring role as the archbishop on CBS's *Blue Bloods*.

"I first did it in a different production in 1988," he recalled. "It was an anthology miniseries re-creating four of Hemingway's novels: *The Old Man and the Sea*, *For Whom the Bell Tolls*, *The Snows of Kilimanjaro*, and an episode about his relationships with his four wives. Looking back, however, I felt that at my age then, just forty-seven, I was too young to do it correctly."

More recently, Keach has been starring in *Pamplona*, a new play different from the one performed by Cariou and Sparks. "This one is the older Hemingway in 1959 when he was commissioned by *Life* magazine to write a piece called 'The Dangerous Summer' and he was suffering from writer's block," Keach said. "He had to confront the demons which haunted him. He was trying to capture the look on Ordóñez's face and couldn't come up with the words."

Keach suffered a heart attack during the opening night performance in Chicago and underwent immediate triple bypass surgery. He said that experience helped him get a perspective on Hemingway's outlook on life when Hemingway realized that his health was beginning to deteriorate. "I felt a fog coming over me as I searched for the words in the dialogue, much the same way as he might've felt, being unable to write."

"I loved reading Hemingway in college," Keach recalled, "and later, I recorded his complete short stories, which also prepared me for the roles. I got the feel of him. I felt I was channeling him. What motivates our play is that it talks about his relationship with women and his deep, deep antipathy to his mother who'd wanted a daughter and dressed him as a girl in his early life. It's a multimedia play with walls moving in and out so it envelops you."

Stacy Keach is no stranger to playing real people: Wilbur Wright, Napoleon, Martin Luther, and Doc Holliday all appear on his fifty-five-year acting resumé. It was when he was playing the tubercular dentist/gambler/gunfighter Holliday in the title role of the movie *Doc* that I met him in 1970. It was one of those magical summers when I was touring with Ordóñez.

Keach, Faye Dunaway, and the other stars of the movie were attending a bullfight in Almería, that dusty small city in southeast Spain. That's the region where many so-called spaghetti westerns were filmed. Ordoñez had one of his great afternoons that day, competing in a *mano a mano* with another great *torero* named Paco Camino. Both matadors had three very brave bulls which needed very little coaxing to charge.

It was a triumphant afternoon, in fact.

Playing Hemingway onstage has come to define the latter part of Keach's career. Whereas he thought he looked too young for that TV performance years ago, now, though seventy-nine, ironically, he looks a decade younger, closer to Hemingway's age.

New York-born Corey Stoll, whose movie credits include *The Bourne Legacy*, *Ant Man*, and *Gold*, portrayed a brash young Hemingway in the ensemble cast in Woody Allen's delightful *Midnight in Paris* back in 2011. It was about a man who gets into an old car in Paris every night, is transported back in time, and meets the luminaries who were in Paris then. It was around the time Hemingway had written *The Sun Also Rises* in 1926. That's when he met Gertrude Stein, her companion Alice B. Toklas, Picasso, F. Scott Fitzgerald, and the other postwar intellectuals who gathered at Stein's legendary Paris salon, the "Lost Generation."

Stoll told me: "Woody Allen had seen me in a production of *A View from the Bridge* at the Cort Theater early in 2010. He contacted me and he would only tell me he wanted to set up a meeting: nothing about an audition. When I got there, he told me he was considering offering me to play a character in his new movie; a 'manly-man' he called it. But at first, he didn't reveal who the character was. By chance, I'd worn my cowboy boots which may have helped the image. Once I realized it would be Hemingway, I was terrified and thrilled at the same time.

"It was funny because there had been another project in development at that time; a movie about Robert Capa, the great combat photographer who was with Hemingway during their coverage of the Spanish Civil War. I began looking up things about Hemingway and thought I could play him in that other movie, but that never came to pass. Woody gave me a few pages of dialogue: the portion where Hemingway was in the big car and was talking about always searching for what is true in his writings."

As was the case with the other actors, Stoll didn't try to replicate Hemingway's voice. "I'd heard his voice narrating the documentary *The Spanish Earth* and Woody warned me not to try that. He said the point of the character is the dialogue, and what it sounds like in the reader's head.

"I had the most fun in that role. I'm really fond of the work I did; that movie was great and magical and very smart. I read Hemingway aloud and nonfiction books about him too. I was trying to get the rhythm and musicality of his writing. Woody didn't give me the entire script, of course—he almost never does with his actors—but when I worked with him again in *Café Society*, he did. I remember the first scene we shot in *Midnight in Paris*, I thought I got it right, but the cameraman noticed a hair in the lens and said we had to reshoot it. But Woody was pleased with my work and said there was no need to reshoot it."

Midnight in Paris is Woody Allen's highest-grossing film to date.

Veteran actor Laurence Luckinbill also portrayed Hemingway onstage. Like Keach, he too had previously played historical characters. There was New Jersey governor Hal Hoffman in the TV movie *The Lindbergh Kidnapping Case* in 1978; then he played three presidents: Teddy and Franklin Roosevelt onstage and Lyndon Johnson onstage and TV in 1987.

"I'd finished playing T.R. onstage in 2002 and toured with it," he recalled to me. "Then I was drawn back to my early self. I was looking for another character to play and thought back to 1961 when I'd heard Hemingway had committed suicide. I remembered I was twenty-six at the time. I'd read all of his works in high school and used the emotional code he'd dug out as a way to live my own life." But Luckinbill, a Catholic, was appalled that Hemingway had taken his own life. "He too was a Catholic, after all, and suicide goes against the teaching of the Catholic faith. So, I remember I banished him from my mind.

"But sometime in 2005, something brought Hemingway back to me. I wanted to find out why he did it; why he committed suicide. It didn't seem to be from early dementia, though that wasn't mentioned back then, in 1961. I knew that his father, a doctor with whom he'd been very close, had also taken his own life. As I began reading about him, I offered to write a play about him for the LBJ Library which had received some of Hemingway's papers. Then the University of Texas suggested I put together a show about Hemingway. Like a crazy person, I agreed to write and star in it."

"After creating a forty-minute script, taking a lot from *A Moveable Feast*, I wrote to Patrick Hemingway, his youngest son for permission. To my surprise he said: 'Absolutely no.' I thought I was risking getting arrested for doing something illegal. But then, Gerald Kennedy, director of the Kennedy Foundation for

Hemingway's letters, said he wanted to produce a play based on the letters. Researching the play, I found a different Hemingway; much more fun; much more self-aware, and eager to live despite the foibles he'd created through his drinking.

"Along the way in my research," he continued, "I found a whole stack of letters to and from his father at the Harvard library. He wrote that he longed to be with his father Clarence, who'd died in 1928 at fifty-seven. His father had written to him a touching note about one of his son's books; it was almost paternal. Dr. Hemingway's son also died much too young. He'd destroyed his body and mind with drink and died trying to find some consolation and he finds it like a reconciliation with his father.

"I decided to take the last two minutes of his life and start there. He'd found the key to the gun cabinet Mary had hidden and took out his favorite shotgun, went to the foyer, knelt down and shot himself. I made a ninety-minute play as an interior monologue—you don't contact or connect with the audience, yet you're looking out at them but can't see them. I knew that earlier plays were based on his speeches and with the actor talking to the audience. I performed my Hemingway play at the Abington Theater in New York and my wife [the actress Lucie Arnaz Luckinbill] made sure I didn't look at the audience.

"It was very difficult to do."

XI

IN NOVEMBER 2016, MY DEAR FRIEND JOE CASTIGLIONE, THE longtime radio voice of the Boston Red Sox, told me he and his wife Jan were planning a trip to Cuba early in the new year. "We're there!" I replied. "We'd love to accompany you. I've always dreamed of returning to the *finca* and what's more—you'll save paying for a translator. I've always wanted to return to the *finca*." He then put me in touch with the Texas Rangers' Hall of Fame announcer Eric Nadel who often conducted tours of Cuba, and Nadel quickly alerted his friends at the Hemingway museum at the *finca* about our impending visit.

In January 2017, we flew from New York to Havana where we were immediately thrust into another world. In many ways there, time has stood still. I hadn't been there since my childhood, but many of the streets looked the same except that nearly every sidewalk we saw in Havana needed to be repaved. The infrastructure is crumbling everywhere. The graying buildings need to be sand blasted, and many people just seem to sit alone in doorways, looking forlorn. Our guide around town was Sigfredo Barón, Cuba's most famous baseball commentator, on television and in print in the national newspaper. "Siggy," as he's called, told us he makes $25 a month, as does every member of the Cuban national baseball team, many with major-league ability. Players, furthermore, aren't allowed to read about their compatriots in this country earning scores of millions of dollars.

The *Finca Vigía* is located near the *pueblo* San Francisco de Paula. There is a watchman's gate beyond which lies a slight incline up a hill. Adjoining the white main house is a guest house which has been converted into an office and where the archives of letters and photographs are kept. A group of several women were there, watching a local game show on a small TV. Then the museum's director at the time, Ada Rosa, returned from giving a tour and gave me copies of two letters my father had written to Hemingway: one from 1940, and another from 1956. Both were excerpted in this book. In exchange, I gave her copies of the photos of my father and mother and the Hemingways, which appear in this book. Then she took us on a two-hour tour of the fifteen-acre farm.

Tourists aren't allowed inside the main house, lest they pilfer souvenirs. We were ushered inside, however. Once inside, you get an astonishingly strong sense of the presence of the man, and even why Hemingway chose that locale to live and write; much more than the home and museum in Key West. The home is breezy and airy and surrounded by dense vegetation.

Nearby, close to the sky-blue walled swimming pool is his fully restored fishing boat, *Pilar* in permanent drydock. It's thirty-eight feet long, with four fishing locations and is perched beneath an open-air canopy to protect it from occasional heavy rainfall. It was named for his second wife Pauline Pfeiffer, as was the main character in *For Whom the Bell Tolls*. Guests on the boat included Spencer Tracy, Errol Flynn, Ava Gardner, and Archibald MacLeish. Gregorio Fuentes, Hemingway's first mate who often steered the boat in tricky waters, is said to have been the inspiration for the character Santiago, the wizened fisherman in *The Old Man and the Sea*. Spencer Tracy played him in the film and Anthony Quinn did as well, in an underappreciated TV movie in 1990.

I remember staring at the reinforced chair from which he fished and came as close as I'll ever come to "channeling" him. You could almost get a real sense of him scanning the horizon for a German submarine conning tower or a periscope jutting just above the water line, waiting to try to blast it out of the water.

Near the *Pilar* was the place I remember most: a small gray cement wall on which stood half a dozen wine bottles of varying colors. Hemingway used that area of the property to practice shooting his .22. As I look back at the short film my parents shot that day, Hemingway seemed to take special interest in me, as the youngest, propping up my arm and holding the barrel of the rifle to steady it, with his left hand steadying on my left shoulder. He quietly encouraged me to be patient before I fired at the bottles. I can't recall exactly, but I like to think my "training" watching countless TV Westerns paid off, and I destroyed the bottle.

Returning to that place sixty-five years later, I also felt Mary's presence. They're all gone now: Ernest, Mary, my parents, and older brothers who so enjoyed that wonderful day. Nearby, I saw the small headstones of the Hemingway dogs. The one in our time there was known as "Black" and I remember him well. There were several sleeping dogs around now, too, descendants of the dogs they kept, along with a slew of cats. It was a tranquil, nostalgic afternoon, the fulfilling of a lifelong dream.

We returned to Cuba in June 2017, this time with our daughter Hannah and her boyfriend Danny Gonzalez, now her husband. I'd been asked to speak at the annual Hemingway Colloquium at the Hambos Mundos Hotel. That afternoon, we returned to the *finca* and saw the new director Isobel giving a tour to some American and Australian visitors. She called me over and asked me, as a "living history person" to speak to the tourists of our friendship with Hemingway and how he changed my life. It was a thrill I will never forget.

In the *New York Times Book Review* section in 2011, the headline for a review of three books about him was "A Swell Life." Was it ever!

High schools aren't teaching Hemingway novels so much anymore, it seems, but he is as relevant today as in his time. Only recently, three of his little-seen stories written in the mid-1950s were discovered. "The Monument," "A Room on the Garden Side," and "Indian Country and the White Army" have been released with a reissue of *For Whom the Bell Tolls*, one of his greatest novels. The manuscripts had been stored in the attic of the Kennedy Library. A fourth story, "Black Ass at the Cross-roads" had been published.

Maybe there are more to be discovered! I hope so.

Jeffrey Lyons

New York, NY August 28, 2020

(The 73rd anniversary of the death in the arena of Manuel Rodriguez "Manolete," Spain's greatest matador of the 1940s, in the town of Linares. A nation mourned.)